Olga took off her skirt and blouse and wrapped herself in her kimono.

"Wonderful," she said. "Now I just wish I had warm feet and my hair pins out of my hair. Then I'd be wishlessly happy."

She rolled an armchair in front of the gas stove and began to unlace her high boots.

"Can I help you?" asked Mette, eager to serve.

"That's all we need!" Olga was ruffled.

"I would not even ask a maid to unlace my boots!"

"That's quite a different matter," Mette smiled. "It's a distinction one would begrudge a maid."

"You are crazy!" Again, Olga's face was suffused with a quick dark flush. Now she had peeled off her thin silk stockings, and she held her naked feet close to the flames. She lifted her arms and slowly pulled pin after pin from her hair until the heavy black strands cascaded down her back.

Lesbians in Germany:
1890's-1920's
Lillian Faderman and Brigitte Eriksson

The Naiad Press, Inc.
1990

Printed in the United States of America
First Edition, 1980
Second Edition, 1990

Cover design by Pat Tong and Bonnie Liss
  (Phoenix Graphics)
Typeset by Sandi Stancil

Library of Congress Cataloging-in-Publication Data

Lesbian-feminism in turn-of-the-century Germany.
    Lesbians in Germany : 1890's – 1920's / [edited] by Lillian Faderman
and Brigitte Eriksson.
        p.   cm.
    Translated from German.
    Previously published as: Lesbian-feminism in turn-of-the-century
Germany. 1980.
    Includes bibliographical references.
    ISBN 0-941483-62-2
    1. Lesbianism--Germany--History.   2. Feminism--Germany--History.
I. Faderman, Lillian, 1940 –   II. Eriksson, Brigitte, 1932 –   .
III. Title.
HQ75.6.G3L47   1990
306.76'63'0943--dc20   89-48962
                                                                CIP

ABOUT THE EDITORS

Lillian Faderman received her Ph.D. in English from UCLA. She is the author of *Surpassing the Love of Men, Scotch Verdict,* two college textbooks on American ethnic literature, and numerous articles on women's relationships. Faderman is a Professor of English at California State University, Fresno and is currently a Visiting Professor of English at UCLA.

Brigitte Eriksson is a native of Germany. She received her MA in English from California State University, Fresno. Her translations include the transcripts of an eighteenth century German trial of a lesbian (*Journal of Homosexuality,* Fall 1979). She is currently a student of Sidda Yoga in Ganeshpuri, India.

CONTENTS

INTRODUCTION

German "Romantic Friends"

In 1805 Bettine von Arnim, a young German woman, wrote to Caroline Gunderode, a woman eight or ten years her senior:

> If you did not exist, what would the world be to me? . . . . I am as good as dead if you do not bid me to rise and live on and on with you. I am certain that my life wakes up only when you call and will perish if it can't continue to grow in you. . . . Yes, my life is insecure; without your love, in which it is planted, it will never come to blossom.

Gunderode returned her passion and need, declaring "you are my bit of a sun that warms me, while everywhere else the frost falls upon me." The lengthy correspondence which exists between these two women suggests an all-consuming love affair in which they provided for each other not only intense affection but also emotional support and intellectual stimulation. Like many English and American women of their day they saw themselves as "romantic friends."

Despite the magnitude of their love, Bettine and Caroline did not live together. Few women did in the early nineteenth century when there was almost no opportunity for women of the middle and upper classes to be self-supporting. They were expected either to marry or to go into a convent or some such female retreat. Caroline Gunderode, the daughter of a widow who had several other daughters to care for, chose the latter and became a canoness in the house of her order.

Of course, the two women might have run off together and become recluses, as did a couple in Britain, Sarah Ponsonby and Eleanor Butler, the Ladies of Llangollen, a generation earlier — but perhaps they were unable or unwilling to risk the fury of their friends and family which the Ladies endured. If they had been born into the lower class one of them might have dressed as a man, gotten menial employment in that guise, and they could have passed themselves off as husband and wife. But to change class at the beginning of the nineteenth century was even more difficult than to change gender — and besides, they might have known of the case of another German woman, Catharina Margaretha Linck, who was burned at the stake in 1721 for attempting to pass as a man and marrying another woman.

But despite the fact that the two did not spend their lives together, their correspondence indicates that, like many other "romantic friends" of the era, they were lovers in every sense except perhaps the genital (and it is unlikely that they would have committed that experience to paper had they had it). To us near the end of the twentieth century it may seem incredible that two women could have loved each other so passionately and never once mentioned their "outcast status" as lesbians or their fear of discovery or the political meaning of their involvement with each other. Such a lack of self-consciousness was possible, however, before the rise of the sexologists in the late nineteenth century who informed the world that there were vast numbers of women who loved other women in ways exceeding the sisterly and that such love was morbid.

The "Invention" of the Lesbian

Significantly, the sexologists emerged in western Europe, and primarily in Germany, not long after the birth of the feminist movement and the start of more plentiful educational opportunities and jobs for women. These expanded opportunities meant that women such as Bettine and Caroline who loved each other could now have the economic and social independence to share their lives, but the sexologists provided fine ammunition for the anti-feminists who were delighted to argue that only masculine women wanted education and jobs and to be masculine was a sure sign of lesbianism, which was sick.

By the early twentieth century, "romantic friendship," unself-conscious love between women, was no longer possible. Once a female left young girlhood she must either transfer all her affections to males or face the fact that she was a "lesbian" and join an outcast society. The sexologists emphasized the sexual aspect of love between women and the unusual, i.e., abnormal, nature of that love. Women were made to understand that if they did not wish to be freaks it was incumbent upon them to suppress any trace of affection for other women, and if they felt strong affection they must recognize that it was genital, which was unclean.

But while the sexologists, who defined love between women as an unfortunate congenital anomaly, scared many women away from the same sex love, by giving concepts and labels to the phenomenon they also made possible for the first time the formation of a lesbian community and subculture. By 1895 some "butch" German lesbians were wearing their hair in the short, curly "tituskopf" bob and sporting tuxedos in the evening and riding pants by day — lesbian styles as distinctive as the ducktails and penny loafers of the 1950s. The word *freundin* (literally: female friend) was coming to connote one's lesbian lover. With the start of the new century lesbians were feeling free enough to exhort others to join them in their novel lifestyle. For example, Marie von Najmajer (a Hungarian-born woman who wrote in German) proclaimed in her poem of 1900, "Hymn to the Daughter of the Twentieth Century:

Good fortune is yours!
Life has prepared a soft bed for you
If gentle woman's love is yours.
You will not be robbed of it in later years,
For it rests not merely on beauty and assets.
However warm and abundant you are, however selfless,
In the same measure you will be paid back.

My child, if what I say seems alien,
Then simply let it be.
But if a light went on in your heart,
Know that you are not alone.
For I live and love love like this,
Such flowers are wound in my wreath.

Anxiously I had been warned all my life,
"Keep silent, do not risk misunderstanding . . .
You are walking at a chasm's edge,
There is danger . . ."

Yet it seems to me
That all of us who are passing through this life
Are walking at a chasm's edge.

As Marie von Najmajer's celebratory poem hints, a woman who agreed to view herself as a lesbian at the turn-of-the-century must have had a powerful streak of social independence and strength of mind. She would have been something of a pioneer. She would not have had easy access to a large social group since there were as yet few clubs or bars where lesbians could meet like-minded women. But as urbanization continued to expand in Germany, so did lesbian social opportunities. Already by 1905 the German pioneer of homosexual emancipation, Magnus Hirschfeld, estimated in his book *Berlin's Third Sex* that there were over a million homosexuals (men and women) living in Germany, and 56,000 living in Berlin alone. Such a burgeoning homosexual population soon gave rise to a number of restaurants, beer halls, and coffee houses which catered to "the third sex," but most of those establishments were primarily for males. The female population remained more covert, although Hirschfeld does refer to a "dating agency" where lesbians in 1905 could make contact with each other and to personal ads which appeared to be directed at lesbians, such as: "Miss, honest, 24 years, is looking for a pretty lady to be her girlfriend." Hirschfeld also describes "masquerade" dances that were held in Berlin, to which "many of the lesbians wear male costumes," and a yearly gala costume party that was organized by a Berlin woman for her large circle of sapphic acquaintances: "After 8 PM on a beautiful evening in winter, myriads of cars stop at the finest hotel in Berlin, and from them emerge ladies and 'gentlemen' in costumes of all countries."

It was not long before unsympathetic critics were complaining about the liberties German women took with each other in public. On February 22, 1909, for example, the *Berlin Daily Blade* expressed its shocked disapproval of a woman performer who had even been arrested because "she sang scandalous songs to entertain a drunken female audience in a cellar bar." The following year the Berlin weekly, *The World on Monday,* exposed a woman's bowling club whose members not only bowled but danced together, some of them sporting short hair, jackets and ties, and even smoking cigars.

German Lesbians and Feminism

Many women who loved other women did not feel comfortable participating in such public revelries. Instead, they found a home in the very serious German feminist movement, which not only helped them affirm their convictions about the importance of female independence, but also afforded them the opportunity to meet like-minded women.

As feminists, lesbians had three main interests: 1) education reforms, which would not only give more women access to higher learning but would also do away with what was then an almost universally accepted notion that girls need to be educated for little else but making themselves pleasant and keeping an efficient house; 2) expanded work opportunities, which would open jobs that had hitherto been closed to females and make independence possible for all women who wished it; and 3) women's suffrage, which, they believed, could and would bring about all other necessary reforms.

While those issues were of concern to many German women in general, to lesbians they were vital. To lesbians of middle class backgrounds they were the *sine qua non* of their ability to live as lesbians without submitting to heterosexual marriage for the sake of maintaining middle class lifestyles. While the term "lesbian-feminist" was not in use at this time, it is an apt description of many of these early German lesbians.

For a long while German "lesbian-feminists" worked in the women's movement without identifying themselves. But at the end of the nineteenth century a homosexual (or — as it was more popularly called — "Uranian") movement emerged, since, ironically, the sexologists who presented same sex love to the world as abnormal also gave those who had the courage to pursue that love a cohesive identity. Though the Uranian movement was comprised at first almost entirely of men, it soon drew many "women-identified-women" and served to raise their consciousness regarding their own rights in the feminist movement. With the strength of the homosexual movement behind her, Anna Rueling was able to point out in a public speech in Berlin in 1904:

> From the beginning of the women's movement until the present day, a significant number of homosexual women assumed the leadership in the numerous struggles and, through their energy, awakened the naturally indifferent and submissive average women to an awareness of their human dignity and rights. . . . Considering the contributions made to the women's movement by homosexual women for decades, it is amazing that the large and influential organizations of the movement have never lifted a finger to improve the civil rights and social standing of their numerous Uranian members.
>
> ("What Interest Does the Women's Movement
> Have in the Homosexual Question?")

Lesbians and the German Homosexual Rights Movement

With characteristic ambivalence, nineteenth century "scientists," after labelling same sex love morbid, generally claimed to be sympathetic to homosexuals. Krafft-Ebing, for example, in *Psychopathia Sexualis,* suggested that homosexuals should not be punished by the law since they were *congenitally* defective and their manner of sexual expression was natural to them, not a matter of exotic choice. Despite the sexologists' ambivalence, some groups within the nineteenth century homosexual rights movement, such as the Scientific Humanitarian Committee, used their "scientific facts" about "congenital burden" in campaigns against anti-homosexual laws, maintaining that punishing homosexuals for preferring their own sex was as unjust as punishing the blind for not being able to see or the lame for not being able to walk. Other homosexual groups, however, such as the Community of the Special believed that this argument would ultimately be self-defeating. Benedict Friedländer, founder of the Community, pointed out "one can certainly pity the diseased, one can behave humanely to the sick and indeed try to 'heal' them; but at no time does one acknowledge presumed physical inferiors to have equal rights." Unfortunately, most homosexual activists of the period were blind to Friedländer's logic. Unfortunately, too, Friedländer's group was essentially anti-feminist: the Community wanted to revive the ideals of Greece, with an emphasis on boy love and comradeship and a total exclusion of women outside of their reproductive roles. Therefore, lesbians who were active in the homosexual rights movement tended to agree with the sexologists that they were homosexual through congenital anomaly. Few would have understood or been sympathetic to the notion of political lesbianism or lesbianism as an existential choice.

Thus, it was the view of the Scientific Humanitarian Committee that became a "party line" for many homosexual women as well as men throughout much of the first half of the twentieth century, even while Freud's equally pernicious theories on the effect of environmental influences on sexual orientation were becoming popular. Radclyffe Hall's notorious English novel, *The Well of Loneliness,* which was published in 1928 and translated into eleven languages, was partly responsible for the longevity of the congenital theory. Hall, too, propagated this theory for reactive political reasons. Through her heroine, Stephen Gordon, who is familiar with the work of Krafft-Ebing and other sexologists who promulgated the congenital theory, Hall argued that since inverts are "born that way," viewing them as "offensive to nature" makes no scientific sense. And because of Hall's popular novel many lesbians throughout Europe and America accepted the theories of these "scientists" as an explanation of the genesis of their "problem" for as long as they continued to believe that lesbianism was a problem.

Perhaps so many women who loved women welcomed the theories of congenital burden simply because it was politically expedient: if homosexuals were born different they could not be culpable under the law; since homosexuality was congenital, society had no need to take preventative measures lest a homosexual try to seduce a non-homosexual — if one was not born tainted one would not be seducible; and if one was born tainted that taint would anyway sooner or later express itself according to the rule of nature. In view of laws against homosexuality that were instituted or almost instituted in nineteenth century Germany, such political expedience seemed to many homosexuals to be the better part of wisdom. Even today in the American gay rights movement many "essentialists" have adopted this ploy.

Until 1794 a Prussian code dictated that both men and women were to be burned at the stake for "unnatural acts," and it was under that law that Catharina Linck was executed in 1721. A "liberalized" code was passed in 1837, so that those found guilty of "unnatural acts" were sentenced only to "imprisonment followed by life-long punishment." In 1851 punishment for "unnatural acts" was restricted by a new code to males only. "Victorian" mentality had spread to Germany. The law preferred to ignore the possibility that women were capable of sexual expression. In 1871 Paragraph 175 of the German Penal Code reiterated that homosexual acts between males were a crime. Later in the century there was some attempt to extend the law again to cover acts between women (as it did in Austria), culminating in 1910 with a new draft penal code. It was at this time — for the first time in history — that feminist groups on a large scale came to the rescue of lesbians. Meetings of women's organizations were held throughout Germany to discuss strategies for fighting the proposed extension of Paragraph 175. The Social-Democrat paper *Forwards* reported that one such meeting of the League for the Protection of Mothers, held in Berlin on February 10, 1911, attracted so many participants that a second meeting was called immediately. The group resolved that it would take the position that extending criminal status to homosexual women was a "serious mistake" and that:

an equality would not thereby be eliminated, but rather an injustice would be doubled. The doors would be opened wide for informers and blackmailers, and unmarried working women who lived with other women would be under a shameful and damaging pressure — while no one's interests would be protected in exchange. At the least, the group believes it is essential that medical experts — particularly sex researchers and psychiatrists — as well as women, be consulted in this matter.

Because of such protest by German women's organizations, legislators defeated the proposed extension of Paragraph 175.

As the works that follow illustrate, German lesbians, from the 1890s to the 1920s, even those who believed themselves to be men trapped in women's bodies, were often feminist in at least some areas of their lives. But there were at that time no organizations that were specifically or exclusively lesbian-feminist. German "lesbian-feminists" of the period often belonged to both a feminist organization and the most popular homosexual organization, the Scientific Humanitarian Committee, which was formed by Magnus Hirschfeld in 1897. According to Hirschfeld, the police sometimes even prevented women from attending the Scientific Humanitarian Committee's public forums because the discussion of homosexuality was regarded as unsuitable in the presence of women. A public lesbian organization would not have been tolerated at that time.

The Scientific Humanitarian Committee set forth as its goals (which were more than half a century in advance of any other country, including the United States): 1) to work towards the abolition of discriminatory laws such as Paragraph 175; 2) to enlighten the public regarding homosexuality; and 3) to enlighten homosexuals so that they will fight for their rights. The Committee held public forums on homosexuality, sent speakers on national and international tours, and provided its publications to governmental commissions studying revision of the penal code. From 1899 to 1923 it published *The Yearbook of Intermediate Sexual Types* and made a concerted effort to include many articles by and about women. Those articles were generally concerned with showing that women too could be born of the "third sex," i.e., that lesbianism was congenital. Hirschfeld was specifically interested in involving "intellectually outstanding Uranian ladies" in the homosexual cause and by 1902 saw them as an "indispensable and prominent component in all our events."

The Lesbian Image, 1890s – 1920s

The most articulate German literary statement about lesbian life at this time was Aimée Duc's remarkable *Are These Women?* (1903).

xvi

Duc's book, while not especially skillful as a novel, has absolutely no peer as an early, emphatically positive "lesbian-feminist" statement — with a happy ending. The rest of the lesbian fiction of the period was written largely by men and often presented lesbians as sick or confused or sinister or all three: in 1900 — R. von Seyditz's *Pierre's Marriage: Psychological Problems* and Jacob Wassermann's *Story of Youth: Renate Fuchs;* in 1901 — Georg Kenan's *Under Women;* in 1902 — Heinrich Mann's *The Goddesses;* in 1905 — Frank Wedekind's *Mine-haha.* Those few novels written by women often depicted adolescent experiences, sometimes by way of warning, as in Maria Janitschek's *The New Eve* (1906) that if heterosexual expression in the young was suppressed, homosexual feelings would surface. More often, these novels depicted teenage crushes between girls or a young girl's innocent passion for an older woman — which were not particularly threatening to the fabric of society, the assumption being that the girl would outgrow this "phase" (e.g., in 1897, Gabrielle Reuter's *From a Good Family* and in 1903, Maria Eichhorn's *Fraülein Don Juan*). A few authors went as far as to suggest, as Reuter did in a later autobiographical work, *From Childhood to Maturity* (1921), that a girlish crush on another woman may be one of the deepest and most serious emotional experiences of a female's life.

The novels about adults often specifically opposed sexual contact between women and suggested that same-sex female relationships must be free of such lowly and ignoble expression (e.g., in 1900 — Elisabeth Dauthendey's *Of the New Woman and Her Love*). And it was not until 1919, with Anna E. Weirauch's *The Scorpion,* the first volume of a trilogy, that lesbian eroticism was more than hinted at in a novel by a woman. Their sensitivity to the possibility of censorship may explain the reticence of many writers of the period. What is more difficult to explain is the existence of a book as revolutionary and ultimately joyful as *Are These Women?*, which neither showed the heroine outgrowing her lesbian attachment, nor suggested that love between women should be asexual, nor hid behind the guise of science.

The works which follow all concern themselves more or less with the problems of lesbians as well as the problems of women. But they are also revealing to the modern reader in what they take for granted as truths about lesbians' emotional make-up and domestic relationships. For example, many of these writers accepted the notion of the lesbian as a member of the third sex, and thus totally different from the average woman. According to Anna Rueling:

The homosexual woman possesses many qualities, inclinations and capacities which we consider masculine. She particularly deviates from the feminine norm in her emotional life. While emotion is almost always — exceptions prove the rule — the predominant and deciding trait in the heterosexual woman, clear reason rules the Uranian woman.

Since social or environmental factors were dismissed as an explanation for rationality, energy, aggression (or the lack of them) as well as an explanation for homosexuality, Rueling and others argued that homosexual women "thought like men" because they were born with men's minds.

Many of these women also took for granted the necessity of a butch/femme dichotomy in lesbian relationships — sometimes because it felt natural to them, sometimes because they were influenced by the rigid nineteenth century division between the sexes and thus believed that two women who were attached to each other had to assign themselves either a masculine or a feminine role in order to make one whole between them. Thus, the "contrasexual" who writes "The Truth About Me" concludes the description of her domestic bliss, "My lovely, dear wife bustles in our cozy home like a true German hausfrau, and I work and care for us both, as an active, vital husband."

Often these writers suffered also from Victorianism (no less strong in Germany than in Queen Victoria's own country), which taught them that while love was noble and the highest good, sex was an evil. Had they been heterosexuals they would no doubt have been just as troubled by eroticism as they were being homosexuals. These women who loved women were still close enough in time to the more amorphous institution of romantic friendship, which had so recently been socially acceptable, to want to cling to it or to want to hide behind it. Mrs. M. F.'s solution to the problem of the "sins of the flesh" in "As I See It" is not to give up her love for women, but rather to replace sensuality with "spiritual nobility and purity," to sublimate it "into creative energy; the ecstasies of my heart take on form and shape. This is how a talent has been generated and come to life." Elisabeth Dauthendey's highly equivocal solution in *Of the New Woman and Her Love* is to present her heroine, Lenore, rejecting the "impure" sexual approaches of sapphists, and finding instead a sensual but clearly non-genital bliss with a younger woman, Yvette:

Without a sound, in the silent ardor of deep, blissful joy, we lay in each other's arms.

And the breath of our beating pulses was just enough to let us speak the beloved name —
"Lenore."
"Yvette."

The two are described as "the blooming young woman in the fullness of her beauty and the mature woman in the fullness of her experience and her immortal hope for the coming life: these two with strong faith in each other, in pure knowledge of each other — united in that devotion with which only women can love." Dauthendey makes it clear that the two women now cling to each other only because men are not worthy of women's pure love, and that when men do become pure themselves noble women such as young Yvette will consent to become wives and mothers. What Lenore will do with the rest of her life and her intense love for Yvette should the latter find the exceptional male, Dauthendey does not say. However, she compensates for this equivocation five years later in a pamphlet called "The Uranian Question and Women" in which she insists, more than sixty years in advance of American women, that feminists have the obligation to lend their support to Uranians.

While lesbians were often trapped into believing myths in the guise of science, they also knew — as puzzling a contradiction as that knowledge must often have been — that they were first of all women, who, even though they chose not to relate to men, were victims of sexism. Therefore, those who thought about the issues were militantly feminist, even to the self-identified masculine "contrasexual" ("The Truth About Me") who suggest that woman — not just those who are "men living in women's bodies," but all women — should be reluctant to marry, because marriage meant "throwing yourself under the yoke" and permitting someone "to assert his 'he shall be your lord and master' upon you"; and who realizes with anger that although she received her primary certificate with the highest grades, she had difficulty continuing her education because she "was a girl."

These women were also among the first to recognize that many a neurotic woman might be cured from her illness, as Minotchka suggests in *Are These Women?*, "if she were set on her own two feet, simply as a human being in her own profession," that the popular female ailment, hysteria, was due to women's prevalent sense of their uselessness, and that if these "sick" women were permitted to do constructive work, almost all of them "would turn into capable, useful persons!"

They criticized their society's assumption that all young girls must and would eventually get married and so needed no career training. They pointed out the terrible injustice committed even by many loving parents who, not having educated their daughters for careers, then believed that since "each girl who was unmarried meant one more mouth to feed . . . best to 'get rid of them' as soon as possible" and thus forced their daughters into dismal marriages.

Best of all, German lesbians often presented an ideal image to those who aspired to be strong new women. This ideal is succinctly described through the character of Minotchka, the heroine of Aimée Duc's novel, a "serious, experienced woman, self-possessed despite her mere twenty-eight years, as only intellectually engaged women are."

By the early 1900s, according to Anna Rueling, the women's movement in Germany appeared to be "advancing unimpeded." Homosexual women felt that they had been silent within the leadership and within the ranks long enough, that it was time that feminists "openly and honestly confess: yes, there are many Uranians among us, and we are indebted to them for their energy and work, which have brought us many great successes," that it was time that the women's movement concern itself with some problems that were specific to lesbians, since lesbians had worked long and hard for the benefit of heterosexual women.

But "lesbian-feminists" would have been unable to make such demands had they not had behind them the strength of the homosexual movement which served to raise the consciousness of lesbians and — despite the pernicious "congenital" theories that some factions of the homosexual movement accepted — served to give lesbians as early as 1900 the first semblance of gay pride. Armed with this pride, the author of "The Truth About Me" exhorts other lesbians:

Take this courage, my sisters, and show that you have as much right to exist and to love as the 'normal' world! Defy this world, and they will tolerate you, they will acknowledge you, and they will even envy you.

This message was suppressed with the rise of fascism in Germany during the 1930s when lesbian meeting places and even private apartments were raided, and some lesbians were committed to concentration camps such as the Buetzow Camp in Mecklenburg.

But before that happened a lesbian subculture developed that, by the 1920s, was unmatched anywhere in the world except perhaps Paris. In Berlin there were about sixty spots where lesbians could go to talk, dance, play, and meet other women — places for middle class lesbians as well as for working class lesbians. There was even an exclusively lesbian newspaper, *The Girlfriend: Weekly for the Ideal Friendship*, sponsored by the Federation for Human Rights (a homosexual organization which, in the 1920s, boasted a membership of 48,000) where lesbian nightspots were openly advertised and where individual women could place their own ads about their desires to meet other lesbians. Such freedom and openness failed to take root anywhere else in the world again for almost half a century.

Lillian Faderman, Brigitte Eriksson
1979, 1989

from   ARE THESE WOMEN?

by Aimée Duc

(Berlin, Eckstein, 1903)

Duc's subjects are college and professional women at the turn of the century. They accept the views of the sexologists with regard to themselves as not women but members of a "third sex," and they even see Krafft-Ebing as a defender of homosexuals because he argued that homosexuals can't help their condition (and therefore shouldn't be punished by the law). A contemporary reader will see that these women are lesbians not because of a congenital drive but because they have taken their feminism to its logical conclusion. The characters view themselves as intellectually elite, and Duc presents them as thinkers and doers in the first excitement of living in an era when finally some women are permitted to be thinkers and doers. Much of the novel is taken up with the discussion of theories about lesbianism and the condition of women. But most astonishing of all for an early-twentieth-century novel, Duc shows these women to be emotionally healthy and she allows the love affair of her central character to have a happy ending.

"The seminar was over. Only a few students trickled out of the university building; the great swarm remained in the corridors. Amongst the first ones who stepped into the street was Minotchka Fernandoff, quite contrary to her usual habit. While she usually never rushed, today she hurried out of the building and down the street with quick steps. Several curious people stopped to look after her. The young woman, strong, well built, voluptuous, looked interesting enough. A mixture of the free-and-easy, the youthful, and the boyish gave her an air of unconscious feminine coquetry and piquantness

1

which permeated her being; it was a special stamp. She wore a black smooth tailored cloth dress, a white stiff collar and wide cuffs. On her thick, curly hair sat a nonchalantly placed plain straw hat; she carried her heavy, yellow leather gloves in her left hand, holding her briefcase with her arm. With the right hand she leaned on an elegant walking stick with a big silver handle. This ever present walking stick attracted attention when she first arrived in the university city; everyone turned to look at her. Nobody guessed the simple reason for this paraphernalia. They all looked for dark and ugly motives. But Minotchka carried the stick partly because she could not climb the steep streets of Geneva without effort and also because she had a periodic weakness in her left ankle.

Minotchka Fernandoff did not seem to notice the stares of the crowd or else she had long gotten used to stares, having accepted the fact that she was unique. Her head raised high, she looked straight ahead. Maybe her gait was too firm and strong for a woman, but this energetic and yet elastic walk fitted with her whole appearance . . ."

Minotchka hurries home because she has invited some friends to a party at her cozy student apartment. Several plates with open-faced sandwiches had been prepared beforehand. There are also wine and beer and cigarettes and several bouquets of overwhelmingly fragrant roses.

The party consists of women students, primarily foreigners: Berta Cohn, from Prague, a zaftig "blonde Jewess with an incredibly kind face. She was still very young, seventeen or eighteen, and nobody could explain why she was already attending the university, but she had passed the required foreigners examination brilliantly. She was taller, heavier and stronger than all the others whom she treated with motherly condescension." *There is also Zeline Ardy, a cheerful, funny Viennese medical student. She is twenty-four and rather pretty but does not care much about her outward appearance. She only cares for science. Then there is Miss Dutier, a French student; Miss Hegerbach, a very poor German student who is tall and thin and terribly young and has the nickname of "Backfisch" (teenager); a Geneva actress and an extremely tall woman from Berlin, Frieda Laube.*

Another guest is "Dr. Tatjana Kassberg, from Little Russia, at that time an intern in the gynecological department of the university clinic. She was a short, nondescript person with a black Titus head, burning eyes and a lively play of feature. A certain cynical, forced frivolity in her character made her not very appealing to the others. Besides, nobody knew anything about her private life, although they tacitly assumed that she was a Nihilist. She also had much intercourse with gentlemen, indeed to be sure with compatriots, but with many who

2

were in no way academic citizens." *There is also* "Frau Annie, a pretty thirty year old woman who had been married for ten years but who had reached an agreement with her husband after six months of marriage whereby he was to give up rights to her property for the use of half of her villa and a considerable monthly payment. He had agreed and in this way they lived their pseudo marriage for the sake of their child who would soon be ten years old. Frau Annie independently managed the large concern she had inherited from her parents; she was a highly esteemed, capable woman who seemed eccentric to the average person.

To her right sat Countess Marta Kinzey, a Polish music student, who was a billionaire's daughter and studied only for pleasure. She was nearly thirty, could not even be called pretty but was distinguished through and through. She inhabited a whole story in a charming villa and was known to be Minotchka's best friend. The fact was that the two had a violent passion for each other and that the Pole had come to Geneva solely because Minotchka had told her during the winter semester in Leipzig that she had decided to go to Geneva."

The repartee among the group is carried on in French, Russian and German. It is explained that "Minotchka, whose father was Russian, a Tartar, and whose mother was French, had been born and raised in France and was actually French. But she felt just as much Russian, and since the women students with whom she was acquainted were mostly German or Russian, all languages were spoken pell-mell. They understood each other excellently."

A certain Elise Fritz is mentioned who recently became engaged. Minotchka is visibly upset.

"Oh go on, the Viennese mocked her: is it because of her that you are so furious? 'Just because she was deceitful!'"

And she cheerfully continued to eat.

'But what should one say,' Minotchka insisted, 'if one of us turns everything into a lie and slaps all our faces — oh, oh!' The countess put her hand lightly on her arm: 'Milaja, Minotchka!' she said gently in Russian, 'Stop. It's important to know what you're doing and especially when you are different from everyone else.' They usually spoke formal Russian with each other in company. Minotchka did not reply. 'My God! So what, if Miss Fritz got engaged,' Dr. Tatjana said harshly. 'I would do it myself if it were necessary for my career! Maybe I'll marry myself an assistant doctor when I start a clinic at home. That doesn't mean one can't keep him at a distance and love whom one chooses. Marrying and loving are two different things after all!'

'But the Fritz woman loves her fiancé,' explained the Jewess.

3

'Well then,' the doctor was bored, 'that means she is a normal being and was mistaken up until then. That's nothing exceptional! Frau Annie, you, dear Minotchka, and I — we all were mistaken at one time, in the opposite way. You both got married first and I had a lover. And then we all had to find out that we have no taste for men and that we belong to the third sex. With the Fritz woman it was the other way around!'

Minotchka was silent. She did not like to talk about her marriage. As a twenty year old student she had married her tutor, a law student, only to get a divorce three years later. She had not recognized her condition before marrying, and marriage with the man who loved her more than anything became a horror for her. When she found herself free once more after three years she revived. Today this time of horror, that pathetic marriage, seemed to her like lost time. 'It was a capital investment for happiness,' she often remarked when she spoke of it.

'That is entirely different,' she insisted. 'The young girl who enters marriage, is still ignorant. The recognition of her inability to accept man as the bestower of happiness does not come until her eyes are opened. But whosoever marries after that recognition is deceitful. Ugh!' And she got up excitedly.

'Well, one's got to try everything!' the doctor laughed cynically.

Minotchka looked at her full of indignation."

Berta Cohn asks Minotchka why she gave up studying medicine for history of literature and then history of art:

" 'I have particular reasons,' Minotchka said quietly. 'You know them as well as I. It's not the fault of medicine that I switched studies but the present condition of science, the suppression of unpleasant revelations! The manner in which one treats woman, be it woman thinking or feeling or not thinking or feeling; that is what made it impossible for me to study medicine. Should I have to treat poor, miserable women and girls whom I could help if I could talk, but with whom I can't talk because science doesn't want to acknowledge what it knows very well? Should I, against my conviction, drive women like me and you into the arms of men only because the world wants to adhere to tradition, because marriage and sexual intercourse between man and woman constitute the foundation of medical livelihood? Can you do that and do you want that? Aren't doctors our worst enemies because they don't unveil truth in the light of science? Couldn't scientific facts steer the woman question into other tracks and show that in addition to the woman question there is also a question of the third sex? And you, who feel as I do, you who are chosen to fight against the arbitrary and traditional, you have the sad courage to be

4

silent? I say 'courage' because I don't have the courage to suffer present conditions in silence. In that respect you surpass me!'

She had become deathly pale; her dark eyes glowed awfully. The countess put her arm gently around her friend and said 'Milaja, Minotchka!' but the insinuative effect of her voice did not work today. The agitated young woman merely squeezed the countess's hand and continued to address the amazed women:

'And you, Dr. Kassberg, Berta and Zeline, would you dare to write a doctoral dissertation about the scientific, positive proof of a third sex? Would you?'

'I'm sure I wouldn't' answered Zeline, 'because no faculty would accept it. But I'll try it someday,' laughed the Viennese, secretly nudging her compatriot from Czechoslovakia.

'My Lord, yes' began Dr. Kassberg. 'Of course you're right in a lot of ways! But how in the world do you want to defend your thesis scientifically? Certainly, there's no doubt that all of us here are inverted women, and there are hundreds and thousands of us. But aren't we perhaps exceptions who can't demand their own laws; aren't we perhaps only strong intelligences whose sex has been put to sleep and maybe killed off and who therefore don't recognize man as such? Who wants to determine this scientifically and how do you want to do that?'

'That is the concern of the psychiatrists,' said Minotchka. 'Although I find it disgraceful that we are classified by psychiatrists. Not even the most nerveless, lowest roué receives this dubious honor.'

'We're well off compared to men,' the doctor interjected. 'Just look at our brothers in suffering and you'll be quite satisfied with our own fate.'

Now the little actress intervened. 'Oh,' she exclaimed in French, 'Oh, how right is Miss Fernandoff. Oh, if only I weren't a poor actress, if only I had studied, oh what I would do! But this way! You have to suffer vulgarities, all men's demands; nobody believes that you live without a boyfriend, that men are nothing to you, and can never be anything to you — oh it is outrageous! How I hate, hate, hate these men, who think they are superior to us, who want us without individuality, without our own spirit, only creatures of their lust. Oh I hate, hate, hate them!'

And she went to Minotchka and leaned her curly head on her shoulder quite exhausted as if finding protection and solace only with her. The debate now became general. All talked simultaneously; the tone became more and more serious, more fervent. A sort of dull sadness lay over the small circle; each and every special interest seemed to have been submerged by the feeling of their solidarity, their fate. The little actress even cried pure tears when she talked about her profession which forced her to depend on the sympathy or even the generosity of men.

The discussion was embarrassing for Frau Annie who, at least for the sake of the outside world, had a husband. Her entire doubtful position in reality and in the eyes of others did not permit her to speak about everything as she would have liked. She got ready to leave. The discussion faltered. The French woman, who had understood only what had been said in French, was obviously bored and so she followed Frau Annie's example. The two Germans also followed along.

Minotchka had accompanied her guests to the stairs. Now she came back into the room. 'Children,' she exclaimed, 'now that we are even more amongst ourselves, we'll have to have another drink!' And she got another few bottles of wine which she emptied into the large decanters.

'Look Minotchka,' said Zeline, finishing her glass in one gulp, 'look, you're quite correct. I'd love to write my dissertation about that subject. Anyway, I have two years to go, and who knows how everything might be changed by then. But now it is impossible to demand the impossible. Even if a few professors would admit this subject, most of them are not yet ready for us! Prosit!'

She said all of this in her soft dialect, in her funny mixture of German and Viennese. She always creataed a reconciling atmosphere, whereas the sharp voice of the doctor created the contrary.

'Certainly,' Countess Kinzey now said, regally calm, 'certainly, we have to try to fight our way into the public, to be acknowledged and not to be ignored! Most people, even the educated, have no idea about our existence, about our needs, our human rights. And yet it's all our own fault! We don't speak up enough, we don't defend our theses, we don't freely reveal ourselves as humans who are neither men nor women. We have to speak up at all times, we have to assert ourselves and we must not let ourselves be intimidated into believing we are sick or let ourselves be forced into an artificial position as specially gifted women who are only grudgingly accepted; we have to make it clear that we are human beings who deserve consideration, since we show ourselves without exception to be an intelligentsia. But we can successfully preserve ourselves only if we step bravely outside the circle of true men and women, if we don't sell ourselves under false pretenses on life's market. Bad enough that we are being forced to play a comedy and to act as women, exposed to everything women have to expect, to be made part of the sample card of wares for men!' 'How

6

true that is, dear Marta, how true!' said the hostess. 'Oh, and couldn't you despair when you see and feel how terribly difficult it is to pretend to be women for the outside world. Certainly, I also say that it is the duty, the sacred duty of each one of us who belongs to the third sex to warn our undecided wavering sisters against marriage, those whose conditions we recognize easily with knowing eyes and the feeling of solidarity, who understand nothing of love; it is our duty to warn them against marriage, to restrain them from making themselves and a man unhappy. If, for example, some compassionate soul had recognized and warned me in due time I would not have robbed three years of life from my former husband and I would not have lost this precious time! Who can measure the torture a woman of our kind finds in marriage! Even the normal but not sensually inclined woman suffers under the sexual marriage union. Such a marriage is the murder of the soul! And how indispensable it is to recognize oneself before marriage, which is a hazardous enterprise for the man as well as for the woman! Marriage is a terribly dangerous venture even for normal people: both sides must agree to it without any guarantee of the other's mental or physical qualifications and therefore marriage suffers shipwreck in so many cases. On these decayed, unhealthy connections the foundation of the state is supposed to rest, love for work and morality are supposed to result from them! Present conditions breed in marriages a proletariat of love which tries to hide under the magic cloak of morality. The result is brutal excesses which violate the personal freedom of one or the other marriage partner. The more the unpleasant consequences of marriage become apparent, the more the brutality increases, which is morally depressing and oppressive. But the worst torture is the esthetic one. For if one or the other partner is constantly offended esthetically, if the smallest, most insignificant action disgusts his sensibility or gives him mental pain which increases to the point of physical discomfort, then marriage turns into a condition of torture, which, without the prospect of release, can lead to raving madness, to murder! Offended esthetic feelings prevent a sexual union or a spiritual union even if social conditions are favorable.'

Minotchka was quiet and looked silently in front of her. If she started talking she let herself get carried away. She spoke convincingly, with enthusiasm; one enjoyed listening to her. Besides, the seriousness of her topic today fascinated every one of these intelligent women.

'You are quite right, dear Fernandoff,' the intern suddenly said. 'We doctors all know that, but we can't publicize it for nobody would want to marry anymore! The largest part of all female nervous disorders and

7

neuroses can be traced back precisely to the marital sex life, which for many women is wrong and coercive. They're left unenlightened about the most natural things and are later laughed at; they are mocked and condemned as "Xantippes," an endless army of hysterical women. Above all, they are held responsible for their condition and they are expected to be self-disciplined, those psychically and physically tortured women. A man in a similar condition is pitied as a neurasthenic; at least he is put into a decent category of sicknesses. The women who suffer in marriage show the most unusual mental anomalies, and any doctor who wanted to see clearly ought to guess the condition of his patients. But we aren't allowed to recognize it for our own good! If one would liberate women from the brutalities of the bedroom, if one set them on their own two feet simply as human beings in their own professions, almost all of these women would turn into capable, useful persons!'

'You know, I believe,' interjected the Viennese, 'that a reasonable person never even gets into such silly love drivel in the first place. A mature mind, cultivated by serious, deep learning, has no room for a love which blinds. When I hear about the crimes, the foolish and ridiculous things which are committed out of love I always doubt the sense of the lovers. Preserve me from being in love!'

'The popular idea of "love," ' mused Minotchka, 'doesn't strike me as being accurate. Because what one has so poetically named "being in love" is never anything but a more or less strongly developed sex urge. I believe that kind of love, "being in love," is actually only a physical pleasure or displeasure. On the other hand, people with a pronounced intellect ought to "love" happily ever after, as they say. I'm speaking only of normal women and men, but I believe nevertheless that a person who occupies himself intellectually very intensively and energetically doesn't have very much time to think about the fulfillment of love. In fact, I maintain that a working person who operates in a healthy equilibrium, doesn't have time for unhappy love; it is a disease for mentally defective people and idlers!'

'I'm of the same opinion,' laughed the doctor. 'The majority of our women suffer from lack of work and intellectual training and therefore become easy victims of unhappy love. This kind of aberration is neurotic and it is high time we put an energetic stop to the unphysiological descriptions in novels and to the hollow, irrational glorification of unhappy lovers and simply treated these people as what they are: namely sick. Continuous unhappy love can seriously endanger life and health and has to be combatted seriously. We have to enlighten the sick; we have to raise their sense of honor and to show them their silly pining in such a way that they recognize their own silliness and become ashamed.'

'Bravo, bravo,' exclaimed the cheerful little woman from Prague, 'bravo, bravo! I'm exactly of the same opinion! Logically considered, love is of value and deserves to exist only when it is shared and only then is it a natural feeling. Yes, yes, love is beautiful when it begins, pleasant, pleasant when it lasts, and ugly when it ends!'

'I don't know whether are right,' said the actress embarrassed. 'I am not an educated, learned woman like you all, and I can't make such beautiful speeches, like Miss Fernandoff. But — according to what has been said before, I ought to have a taste for being in love! And yet it is not so. I believe that this is due to my own nature. Women like us can never love man as man. But I'm sure there are also real women who love in different ways too, and this is why I think it is so misleading to call all the various feelings of sympathy or attachment "being in love"! I believe that being in love makes you unfree, and I think that the highest good is to maintain the freedom of one's self!'

Dr. Kassberg clapped her hands vigorously. 'Just look at our Pierrette!' she mocked. 'Our chrysalis is turning into a butterfly!'

And she patronizingly stroked the actress's hand."

It has become late and the party breaks up. The countess is the last guest to leave. She hugs Minotchka, kisses her hair and whispers to her that she is expecting her at her place tomorrow.

Minotchka and the Countess decide to spend semester break in Interlaken and have several relaxing weeks together. When they return to Geneva they both find unpleasant news. The Countess's old father has fallen ill and wants her to hurry to Aix-les-Bains where he has gone to take the baths. Minotchka has a letter from a Russian friend who is deathly ill and asks her to come to Clarens in order to help take care of some final business. There is also one more letter from a certain Dr. Laum who had adked Minotchka to marry him shortly after her divorce. She had told him no. Apparently he now wants to renew his efforts.

Minotchka goes to see her dying friend and helps her straighten out her affairs before her death. When she returns to Geneva, Minotchka feels very low and misses Countess Marta Kinzey intensely. She has an indistinct fear that her friend might stay away longer than had been planned. Minotchka also finds a calling card from Dr. Laum. She wishes she would not have to face him alone. Just then Frau Annie and Boris Karaschneff, a medical student, the only male friend Minotchka enjoys seeing at any time, arrive. He very much admires Minotchka without letting her notice his feelings and he is actually jealous of every man she knows. That is why he delights in taking part in the following interchange with Dr. Laum.

Minotchka greets Dr. Laum very graciously and serves sherry. Dr. Laum proposes a toast and tells Minotchka he hopes to see her happy at the side of some beloved man.

"He had done the most disadvantageous thing in this situation. Nothing outraged Minotchka, with her strong, independent nature, more than the constant pointing out of man as an attribute of happiness. She always felt this to be an insult, an underestimation of her value, and due to her temperament, she became inconsiderate, even rude.

'Dear Doctor,' she said urgently, 'let me tell you one thing. Stop those phrases of yours! I don't want to hear them, once and for all! As much as I enjoy you visiting me as an old friend, could you ruin this hour for me if you don't speak sensibly!'

'But my dear Mrs. . . . !' he stammered utterly confounded.

'Don't call me that!' she exclaimed, now really indignant. 'Just as I gave up the name of my former husband when I was divorced, I stripped off everything else. I am simply the student Minotchka Fernandoff!'

'Well, what should I call you?' he asked genuinely afraid.

'Miss or Mrs. Fernandoff,' she mocked. 'Whichever you find prettier.'

The doctor was obviously undecided whether he should leave or stay. But he noticed that Frau Annie, who had no idea of the visitor's plans, looked at her companion disapprovingly. This made him decide to stay. He swallowed his ill humor and asked divertingly: 'How is Miss Zeline Ardy? Where is she living?'

'Zeline went to Zurich for this semester,' explained Minotchka, happy to give the conversation a new direction. 'And what is your sister doing? Is she still at the Leipzig conservatory?'

'Oh no,' the doctor replied, 'she wasn't supposed to study music! She took lessons just to pass the time, just like all young girls pass the time until they can fulfill their real calling.'

'Is your sister engaged, then?' asked Frau Annie for politeness' sake and because she saw that Minotchka was ready with a sharp reply.

'Oh no,' he said naively, 'but she hasn't given up the hope of marrying; she's only twenty-four years old. At the present time, several gentlemen are interested in her; I'm sure that one or the other will come through. Since we are orphans, Marianne is presently staying with an aunt.'

10

'Good heavens!' exclaimed Minotchka, jumping up. 'How disgraceful! Do none of the young girls today have any honor left?'

The doctor was taken aback.

'How do you mean that?' he asked unsure of himself.

'How do I mean that?' Minotchka mocked. 'Well, that's not too difficult to understand! I find it dishonorable and degrading to raise a girl from childhood on for marriage without recognizing her individuality, and to train her for the man hunt instead of offering her the choice of an honorable livelihood. Don't you feel that you insult your sister when you say that she's still hoping that something will come up? In other words, she would take anybody, if only someone would come?'

The doctor felt increasingly uncomfortable and didn't know quite how to answer.

'But all women should and do want to get married, don't they?' he insisted once more.

'Should and do want to?' Frau Annie seized the expression. 'No, doctor, that is not quite right! Not all of us want to marry, nor should or will all of us marry in the future! For we are first of all human beings and only then breeders. All breeders are humans, I suppose, but not all humans are breeders.'

'I don't quite understand you,' said the doctor. 'Even if not quite all women shall and do want to get married, there's nothing else they can do. A girl can't be a burden to her parents or relatives forever! Isn't it awful to become an old maid?'

'Certainly,' replied Minotchka, 'it must be horrible to be an old maid whose humanity has been extinguished, and whose life is nothing but a demoralizing parasitism. First the parents have to feed the reject much longer than they wish; then the brother or brother-in-law plays the part of the provider; then the relatives, and, if they don't own anything or if there aren't any relatives, the community, the state has to take care of the sick old maids. Fortunately one does not yet let them die on the street; that is worth a lot,' she mocked.

'In Russia they share your opinion,' Boris now entered the conversation. 'We call such old misses "Prischiwalka," that means one who moves from place to place for bed and food!'

The good-natured mockery of the Russian annoyed the doctor. 'All right,' he said, seemingly calm, 'that might be as you say, but I still believe that only emancipated women are against marriage and in favor of a career. And we must not be guided by them because emancipation is in its true essence a negation of marriage! Unfeminine women are a horror for everyone, aren't they?'

11

'Without a doubt!' said Minotchka.

'Well then?' asked Laum, full of amazement.

'We merely understand different things when we speak of unfeminine women,' she observed. 'For what is this concept "femininity"? A wish dictated by man in order to mold woman according to his taste. Therefore, we are confusing cause and effect if we believe women whom men think very "feminine" to be so. Quite the contrary. They are the "unfeminine" since they live only for the wishes and pretensions of men. Consequently, the really "feminine" ones would be those who keep their individuality all for themselves and who form a special species, physically and psychically. Certainly, woman as mother is "feminine" and beyond any commentary. But no woman thinks immediately about motherhood when she wants to win a man for herself.'

'Yes, but how do you define so-called femininity?' Laum asked, growing more interested. 'What is your idea?'

Minotchka had folded her hands in her lap and contemplated them. 'I have my own design,' she smiled. 'I start with the assumption that every healthy female being ought to be trained for a profession, just like a man. Each one according to her talents. Some would become crafts people, others would devote themselves to trade, others to office jobs, to university studies, to teaching, to art! Later on, the different factions would part without hatred, some in order to find their happiness in marriage, others who don't feel like it, to stand on their own feet as free persons. This would not involve any risk because a person's inclinations would decide, and the number of those who want to marry will always be greater than that of the others. However, countless women would remain liberated from the marriages which would be torture for them and into which they are now being forced; marriage, on the other hand, would profit since only those who are favorably inclined would enter the marriage state.'

'But I believe that many women marry because they don't want to work, or let's say because they don't have the courage to stand up for themselves!' said Laum.

'Certainly,' agreed Frau Annie. 'More than one thinks. But that is the result of bad education. It's necessary to have courage in order to go through life today as a woman and to obtain adequate job security.'

'I agree with my friend,' added Boris.

'I too believe that each woman ought to be trained for a profession according to her capabilities and talents, her social condition and her state of health. Only this way will she later be kept from grave psychological conflicts. Education, of course, would only be an

12

introduction to professional life and only when you have completed your education should the free choice of a career become your right. For marriage isn't a specific career for either man or woman but merely a safety valve designed by the state!'

'Oh my heavens,' protested Laum, 'then women would become our competitors in all fields!'

Minotchka laughed loudly and clapped. 'Naturally!' she quipped, 'and *what* competitors. Even Cato said: "As soon as women become equals they would become stronger than we and would subjugate us!" You see?'

'I don't doubt women's capabilities,' the doctor replied, 'but I want to say that man's fight for existence will be emphasized through woman's competition and that it will be increasingly difficult for him to marry.'

'An eternal, vicious cycle,' said Minotchka. 'Certainly, the competition of women is to be feared, but my principle is: the right of the stronger, not the physically but mentally stronger! Whether man or woman — only intelligence has rights, not sex! Capability must decide. Certainly, each day and each year the fight for existence is becoming more difficult because of the increasing refinement of mental capacities. Each person has to fight hard in order to achieve even a little. And in order to hold on to what he has gained he has to be constantly ready to fight so that no one else gets ahead of him. Let us finish fighting this battle, dear doctor — intelligence is trump!'

'You speak excellently,' the doctor laughed with a sour-sweet expression, 'but with your theories you leave life no sunny sides! If all of us wanted only to struggle then all of life's outward beauties would be lost; there would remain only one realization for us: that life is only work, work and livelihood! But mere work and gain, whether in higher mental realms or in manual labor, cannot possibly replace poetry and happiness!'

'Not at all,' replied Minotchka. 'you throw out the baby with the bath water! On the contrary, I hope for many more of life's beauties if I assume that all humans delight in creating, that to each the paths are open which will lead her to do research and gain knowledge and which will make it possible for her to use her strength and intelligence and according to her individual nature and her inclinations obtain those beauties of life which particularly entice her.'

'I also believe that you have forgotten what you said before,' continued Frau Annie, 'you want to make women, as the most beautiful beings, the center of life and you think that we want to rob you of this idea. However, we emphasized expressly that most women

13

will always decide in favor of marriage, a marriage perhaps, which has been sealed under more dignified, purposeful conditions. But on the other hand we want to leave each woman her own intellectual and physical freedom and also preserve for ourselves, who aren't breeders, our human rights!'

'Right,' said Laum, 'what you say is completely justified! But I'm only afraid that woman is going to change more and more in the course of time, and that finally, when we want to marry we'll have to eat in a restaurant with the wife, and that woman as "guardian of the hearth" will soon become a myth. With such a lack of domesticity all social life in the house, in the family, would come to a halt! The word "housewife" will then soon be completely devalued.'

'My God yes, modern times and progress cause all this anyway!' explained Frau Annie. 'Our social life today has become different, freer. It demands and offers more than in former times while relieving the woman. The public restaurants beckon not only to the man but quite frequently also to the woman: married couples take their meals together in restaurants and read their newspapers! Meet their acquaintances! One doesn't have to make any concessions to society because of it; one comes and goes as one pleases! and then,' she continued, 'how pleasant, for example, to give a large festivity or party outside the house. Almost all my friends do that! You save so much in excitement, discomfort and responsibility! And the woman for whom each festivity becomes a torture because of the work and the preparations is especially relieved this way. Look, Dr. Laum, it's really very practical: You invite your friends to a hotel; the uncertainty about what to offer and the inadequacy of servants are eliminated, and besides — the pleasure is much cheaper and you return to your house which remains unchanged. No confusion, no upheaval, the housewife goes to the party like all other guests!'

'But you have to admit,' exclaimed Laum, 'that this way the woman will lose all ideal value in the home, if one ignores the practical value. The domestic hearth will become more and more monotonous, boring and neglected.'

'Yes, to be sure,' replied Minotchka, 'because even today it can't compete with what is being offered by the outside world. Public entertainment is slowly but surely drawing the modern world under its influence.'

'The devil take it,' the doctor laughed half seriously, half amused, 'it would be stupid to marry!'

'Certainly,' 'naturally,' 'but that's what we say too,' the answers resounded." *Dr.Laum, probably realizing that he does not have a chance, takes leave. Minotchka shakes his hand warmly and assures him that she will always love to hear from him.* When Boris makes fun of the visit, Minotchka turns to him sharply and tells him that she will not tolerate any ridicule in regard to Dr. Laum. *The Russian remains silent. Frau Annie asks whether Minotchka wants to come to the "Terrassenkonzert" she is planning to attend this evening. The three friends decide to go together.*

"The evening was delightful. Those who were able to went outdoors. The concert terraces were crowded with visitors. All the tables were tightly packed and between the rows moved a cheerful, chattering mob. The three companions looked for empty seats. Just then somebody called them. At a large corner table sat their friends, Dr. Tatjana Kassberg, her cousin Mischah Stetsky, a Russian woman dentist whose university studies everyone doubted but not the fact that she was Mischah's lover, Berta Cohn, the actress and Dr. Rentor, a young German woman who was just as serious as she was learned. On the table sparkled a large punch bowl; everyone seemed to be in an extraordinarily gay mood. 'Well,' said Boris, who immediately suspected something extraordinary, 'what is happening here?'

Everyone spoke at once, but the Jewess' voice rose above them. 'Tatjana was appointed assistant doctor at the clinic today,' she shouted. 'She is taking the position of Miss Reuter, who is going to Bern as first assistant doctor!' " *They congratulate Tatjana, sit down with her, and the conversation is resumed. Someone asks Minotchka about her beloved countess and whether she is planning to return soon. The question disturbs Minotchka. She replies that she has no idea since her friend has not yet written.*

After some time, Pierette, the young actress, asks Minotchka to come into the garden because she has something important to tell her. Minotchka is not overly thrilled because she does not care for women like Pierette who are timid and seemingly without energy. With them she always becomes abrupt, almost brutal.

Pierette asks Minotchka whether she really is planning to go to Germany for the summer semester. When Minotchka answers positively, Pierette asks whether she can come along. She is determined to leave the stage because she can no longer stand the life connected with it, and she hopes to make a living teaching French and giving piano lessons. She is afraid to do it all on her own. Minotchka is surprised and then won over and tells Pierette to be ready by March. Pierette is overjoyed; she kissed Minotchka's hand and cries that Minotchka can do what she wants with her, for she is so grateful. But Minotchka tells her to restrain herself. She merely wants to watch over her until she had become fully independent. She advises Pierette to learn some German.

When they get back to their table, they notice that two gentlemen have taken away their seats. Minotchka asks why her friends let them sit down and is told that the gentlemen were going to leave as soon as the ladies returned. The strangers get up; one protests politely. When Dr. Rentor, Mishah and the dentist get ready to leave and offer their seats, the two men decide to stay.

The little circle resumes its conversation. Gradually, their mood heightens and they become more and more animated. Suddenly the strangers join the conversation.

" 'I take it you are studying medicine?' one of them asked Dr. Kassberg quite abruptly. He had guessed this fact from the general conversation.

'I am a doctor, yes!' she uttered reservedly.

'Oh, that's extraordinarily interesting,' one of them said, 'We are German. Professional women are still a rarity in our country.'

The gentlemen briefly introduced themselves, one talked more or less accurately about this and that and also about women in private and public life. And quite unexpectedly the younger one of the gentlemen asked Tatjana: 'Tell me, mademoiselle, doesn't the presence of women in the hospital lead to all sorts of romantic occurrences?'

He said this with a meaningful wink.

'Not at all,' was the short reply. 'The seriousness of the situation leaves no room for the non-essential.' The questioner felt himself to be put in his place but that only incited him to further discussion. He tried to put her in her place by saying, 'But I believe that a woman who has spent years in the university, in hospitals and the anatomy lab can't possibly retain the charm of woman. She must become serious and harsh, dogmatic and pedantic, arrogant in the sense of her own importance, and, as man's rival, incapable of love as well as of friendship. She will be able to see in man only a competitor and, since he is better equipped for battle than she is, an enemy!'

'Is that all?' asked Tatjana.

'No,' the other one continued zealously. 'I believe that an educated woman, a woman who has gone to the university, is not fit for marriage, because she will put her studies above her household!'

'Of course,' said Minotchka, 'that's exactly why we won't marry! I completely agree with you that the sensitive, devoted feminine woman can never become a doctor nor will she accomplish anything else

16

significant in public life. These women belong in the home and also they will like it best in the home. Please don't confuse us with these very valuable women, who should be highly esteemed — we belong to a different category!'

'Yes, but my heavens!' the elder gentleman said thoughtfully, 'but you are women, aren't you? And when woman seriously tries she'll always find work according to her strength! For example in nursing!'

Minotchka's chair shot around. 'You forget one more thing,' she said coldly. 'Two professions are always open to woman: nursing and — prostitution! The one profession offers only self-negation, patience and suppression of individuality and suffering in the name of faith, and the second secures for women an ancient trade through the abandonment of their bodies, a trade which they are permitted to follow without objection.'

The gentlemen fidgeted restlessly.

'Those who have the capacity for subjugation, tolerance and faith should become nurses and those who don't want that — whores!' Minotchka continued harshly. 'That's just about the alpha and the omega of life. And in between fits marriage!'

'That isn't what we mean,' the stranger interjected vexedly, 'but one ought to marry; every woman ought to find a husband.'

'Please,' Boris mocked, 'why don't you introduce polygamy?'

'That's not what we want at all!' the speaker resisted.

'It is not at all to be discounted,' said Dr. Kassberg. 'I lived amongst the Ormans for a long time and I have to admit that women's lack of liberty amongst the Moslems is not any worse because of polygamy than in the Occident because of an apparent freedom. Only the wrapping is different.'

'Yes, that's how it really is!' Boris agreed, 'here as there women sell themselves for a guarantee for board and room! But for the same service, the oriental woman is at least insured against expulsion and desertion.'

'We are getting off the subject,' said one of the gentlemen. 'Concerning the question of college, Lombroso too believes that mental work, the strenuous higher activity ruins the nerves of women. Just look at all the hysterical women!'

'But my dear sir,' the doctor said emphatically while she stirred her coffee nonchalantly, 'you judge merely as a layman! You merely repeat what you have heard! As a doctor I want to tell you that most of the hysterical, neurotic, so-called misunderstood women are married women who have almost without exception become victims of psychic disorders because the lack of productive, satisfying activity, of

17

intellectual enlightenment, of mental training is taking its revenge. Strengthening of the will and education of the mind are the best prophylactic means for avoiding hysteria. The love madness of hysterical persons hardly ever evolves from a strong sensual need but from a morbidly agitated imagination. Even our famous Prof. Dr. von Krafft-Ebing says that "these women love only as a compensation, in order to make up for their mental loneliness; desire has much less to do with it"!'

The elder of the strangers laughed mockingly. 'Thank God we don't understand your views! But à propos Krafft-Ebing. Isn't that the one who defends perverts?'

Proudly he looked around the table.

'Of course,' said Minotchka, 'he is the one, the author of the work *Psychopathia Sexualis,* which most laymen and uninformed approach full of greed, curiosity and lust!'

The companions laughed secretly; the strangers made no reply. Then they whispered with each other, paid the waiter who just happened to pass by and got up.

'Good evening!' they said politely but coldly to the whole table, as if they had never exchanged a word with them. Everyone laughed.

'We chased them home!' Berta Cohn said jubilantly.

'Too bad,' said Minotchka. 'I would have liked to have initiated them further! I wanted to tell them that we too belong to those "Krafft-Ebing types!" I believe they would have fainted!' "

The countess returns after some time and the two friends spend several wonderful weeks together, studying, celebrating Christmas, carnival. Suddenly one day, the countess comes to Minotchka with the news of her father's death. She has to go to Warsaw to take care of the estate. Before they part, the two women promise to remain faithful and to wait for each other.

The following semester, Minotchka, Boris and Pierette go to Munich. Minotchka finds music students and a part-time governess position for Pierette. She avoids the little actress who has an enormous crush on her as much as possible. All her thoughts are for Marta Kinzey, who writes long letters at first and then only short postcards; then a letter in which she tells Minotchka how much her father's death has exhausted her and that she will go to a North Sea island to recuperate. Why doesn't Minotchka come and join her? If that is impossible, they will meet again in Munich next winter.

Despite the countess' emphatic assurances of her love and her great longing for her friend, Minotchka has a feeling of disappointment and emptiness. She throws herself into her studies, then joins a bowling club and "frequently undertook again big bicycle tours, and at this opportunity had met a small bicycle society which consisted of two baronesses von Blum, several painters and a law student. They were all independent women who publicly confessed belonging to the third sex. And with renewed vigor Minotchka discussed her favorite subject with them. They often visited the Löwenbräukeller in the evening, where the little group had very serious discussions while drinking the magnificent beer and listening to music. At one time they discussed the situation of women in Germany, their suppression and the obstacles that are put into the way of their desire to learn. Nadine, who had also gone to the university, told of her experiences and concluded that she thought that German women were less capable of taking up a scientific profession than any other women, of any other nation. 'That I don't believe!' Minotchka had replied excitedly, 'because in view of today's successes and the tireless progress of feminists we have to be respectfully amazed that German women through the generations preserved so much intelligence in order to be able to fight the hard battle for knowledge and professional freedom. We have to be amazed that they were mpt tirmed into idiots and mental cretins by the intellectual fast-cure to which they have been subjected. In this case, woman is, despite apparent stagnation, far ahead of man in whose path nobody steps hinderingly when he wants to satisfy his intellectual hunger. Woman, however, stands in front of a gate, and up until now only few tough natures have succeeded in climbing over that high gate and looking on the other side of the obstacle for the appeasement of their intellectual hunger.' "

The discussion gradually develops into an argument against marriage, against love.

The semester approaches its end. The countess seldom writes. Finally, Minotchka receives a very cursory, hasty letter in which Marta Kinzey describes the isle of Sylt and speaks much of a young, sick officer who is very musically gifted. She describes his piano playing in detail. Of Minotchka and herself she speaks very little. The vehement protestations of love at the end of the letter seem deliberate and contrived. The letter fills Minotchka with a dull fear and apprehension. She experiences a feeling of hatred toward the strange officer.

A few weeks pass. Finally another letter arrives. Boris is with Minotchka when she reads it. She is seized with despair, loses her mind momentarily, is shaken with uncontrollable sobbing, then after several hours regains her outward composure. For four weeks she refuses to see anybody. Apparently she never leaves her rooms. Her landlady tells Minotchka's friends that she is deeply involved in scientific work and wishes not to be disturbed by any interruptions. Since her friends are used to her abrupt behavior, they leave her alone.

One evening she unexpectedly appears again in the group. Not even the sharpest observer could detect any difference in her appearance. When all have gathered she makes an announcement:

"'My dear companions! I have to inform you that one former member, the Countess Kinzey, will not return into our circle as one of us, neither to Geneva, nor to Munich, nor anywhere else! Six weeks ago she married an officer in Leipzig!'" *Suddenly, Boris understands Minotchka's behavior during that frightening evening weeks ago.*

Minotchka never mentions the countess again. Only once does she visit the circle. From then on she remains solitary. During the semester break she goes off alone without telling anyone her whereabouts. She promises Pierette to return to Munich, although her young ward has found a full-time position as governess in a professor's family and has become a different, cheerful person, content with her new career.

Two years pass. The former circle has been dispersed, Minotchka is thinking of leaving Germany. She plans to go to Australia to become director of an international finishing school. Deliberately she chooses exile to separate herself from the country which contains so many painful memories for her.

Before she leaves she has a sudden longing to see Paris once more, to revisit the site of her childhood and youth and to spend April in Paris. Once in Paris, she is seized with the ecstasy of hearing and speaking her mother's language. She explores Paris, visits her childhood neighborhood and suddenly comes to the exciting decision not to leave France. She is going to stay in her home and, for the first time in years, she is exuberantly happy. She sends a telegram to the school in Sidney, informing them of her change in plans.

Minotchka stops to greet a flower vendor who recognizes her after ten years' absence. No longer is she the giddy young girl who left a decade ago, but she is a "serious experienced woman, self-possessed despite her mere twenty-eight years, as only intellectually engaged women are." *She buys a bouquet of flowers just to be buying something from the old woman. When she becomes aware of what she has chosen — a large clump of white, star-like pansies — she realizes that these used to be Marta Kinzey's favorite flowers. They were in her rooms during all seasons and she always wore a small bouquet in her belt. Minotchka is overcome with painful memories. She decides to think of something else, to leave her youth behind and concentrate on the here and now. She goes for a walk in Père Lachaise cemetery, enjoying the peace and the abundance of flowers which cover even the poorer graves. Everything is peaceful, beautiful and quiet.* "Then a lady came around the crossroads; undecided, she stood for a moment before walking down the street in the same direction as Minotchka. The stranger wore mourning clothes, but with a certain cheerfulness which showed anything but sorrow. And with an ironic, bitter feeling Minotchka thought that one couldn't put as much piquant coquetry into any other clothes in the world as into mourning clothes. The woman walking in front of her wore a flower-like black silk crepe dress which she was gracefully holding up so that one could see a medley of lace, ruffles and flounces. The black palettes on the hat sparkled in the sun and the parasol looked like a big bouquet of black roses and lace. The stranger wore her hair in thick short-cut strands of curls, and — 'Marta,' Minotchka murmured involuntarily. All the blood rushed to her heart: that was the walk, the figure, the posture of the countess, and most of all, the hair, the strange blonde hair! She hesitated for a second — she felt as if she had to hurry after the stranger, as if she had to look into her face; then she resolutely turned away into a side path. Was she suffering from hallucinations today, thinking that she saw the lost friend everywhere and in everything? For such a long time she had been lulling herself into a seeming forgetfulness and now everything was awakening again at such an inopportune time, just when she had to begin a new life! Why ever had she bought those enticing pansies? It was their fault; they had steered her thoughts back to the past and had awakened memories! To the side stood a dilapidated, badly kept grave. An abundance of wild violets grew between the evergreen and the light green spring grass. With a sudden movement, Minotchka put the flowers on the strange grave. 'Just peace, peace,' she murmured, 'it is better than happiness!' For a long time she stood motionless before the colorful mound; with difficulty she found her way back to reality. The air was full of fragrance and heavy, a ringing and weaving everywhere — peculiar to beloved spring — the clouds hurried so quickly in their dizzying height — and she was so tired, so tired and so comfortably languid.

She walked a few steps to the next bench. Resting felt so good! Suddenly a grating of the gravel, a rustling of a woman's silken dress — Minotchka looked up. There she was again, the stranger, she came toward her . . . and suddenly, with a shriek the black-clad lady sank down in front of Minotchka. She clasped her motionless friend and murmured with suppressed sobbing, hoarsely, tonelessly, 'Minotchka, Minotchka!' Then Minotchka shook off the anesthetizing feeling which had seized her and, grasping the kneeling woman, she asked vehemently: 'Marta, Marta, is it really you?' The other looked up. A world full of pain and full of love shone on her face. 'How did you get here? How in the world did you get here?' asked Minotchka incredulously. 'And where, where is — your husband?' She managed to get the words out only with a strain; it seemed to cost her great pain to collect her thoughts.

'But he is dead,' said Marta, 'he's been dead for half a year. Back there in Davos, they buried him! Since then I've been wandering around, without any plans; aimless! I haven't given up hope of finding you somewhere, although I wouldn't have dared to look you up! Milaja, Minotchka, won't you forgive me?'

But she received no answer. With a strangely fixed look the other stared out over all the countless graves.

'Just listen to me, Minotchka,' begged the Pole, 'don't be so apathetic! Look, I've never forgotten you. Here in the face of the dead I swear to you! I've never been anything but a friend to my husband! What brought us together was music! He knew everything about me and yet he wanted me for a wife for the sake of outward appearances; he wanted to be my companion, my comrade. Oh Minotchka, and how I suffered despite his love and kindness, how terribly did fate revenge itself — it took its revenge on you, if you will! No, women of our kind must not marry, not even in friendship; it is against all nature! Such a marriage is a poor, nameless relationship, a fetter, a rape, an outrage, in the lightest case a terrible burden! Oh, you don't know how I have suffered! And you, you, who are so just, so firm, you want to judge now? Can't you forgive me? Can't you let the past rest?'

She pressed Minotchka's hands anxiously. 'I'm afraid,' Minotchka said dully, 'I'm afraid of a second disappointment! I can no longer be trusting and open.'

'But beloved,' the Pole begged, 'beloved, be reasonable! Don't barricade yourself behind your pride which robs you of everything! Is not erring human? And did you not err yourself? Do you want to condemn me who gave to a man only her friendship? Couldn't it be like before? Look, even married couples separate for long times out of some terrible error, only to stick together ever closer afterwards. Couldn't we do the same? Can't you bridge the past, can't you believe me anymore? Come to Warsaw with me: my estate is close by. I'll lead you through the laughing sun and the golden wheat fields! There we'll complement each other. There you'll once again be my beloved tyrant and I your obedient Marta. I will worship you and serve you and I will expiate a thousand-fold what I unknowingly inflicted upon you! And in the fall we'll return to your homeland until the warm sunshine calls us back into my country once again. Do you want to set out on this

22

new venture with me, will you trust your life to me? Minotchka, do you still love me?'

Then Minotchka bent down to her kneeling friend, and pulling her up she said merely, 'I want to.'

And they walked arm in arm toward the city, out into the bliss of spring and of their lives!"

THE TRUTH ABOUT ME

by E. Krause

(from *Yearbook of Intermediate Sexual Types,*
Volume III, Leipzig, 1901)

Like so many lesbians of her era, the author of this essay was the oldest child of her family and allowed to grow up unimpeded by sex role stereotypes. She carried the freedom she enjoyed as a child into adulthood. Her first serious jolt out of the bliss of that freedom came when she realized that despite her talents, she could not go to the school of her choice because she was a female. Because of such outrages against women, she learned to identify completely with the masculine, and, as the sexologists taught women of her day, she attributed loving women to her masculinity. But her essay is remarkable because her joyous, positive temperament and her view of herself as a success in life shine through in spite of her morbid "medical" indoctrination.

Autobiography — self-adulation — one should keep one's hands off it. And yet I'm not going to. Why not? Because I've repeatedly been asked to serve the good cause by telling the truth. Nevertheless — I'm afraid, afraid!

I'm by no means one of those who are unhappy about their condition, who hang their heads and want to tell everyone: "Oh, we poor deviants! Pardon us for existing!" No, I am proud of my exceptional state, I boldly raise my head, stand up proudly and say: "Look, this is me!"

I was born in a small town, the daughter of a scholar and the oldest of eight children. I'll refrain from discussing whether I'm hereditarily burdened or not for the time being; for, although I know a little about the noble science of medicine, I don't feel called upon to write a learned treatise at this point. Perhaps sometime later.

My youth was spent like that of all boys, who enjoy the marvelous advantage of simultaneously experiencing the freedom of country life and the pleasantness of the city, an advantage which is possible only in a small town. When I say that I lived like the boys, I deliberately use this expression because, first of all, I felt completely like a boy even then, and secondly, I was lucky enough to receive a complete boy's education.

How sorry I felt for the poor girls, who had to trip along "modestly and well behaved" with briefcases and music scores under their arms, while I wrestled and raced with my wild comrades, cheeks glowing and hair flying in the wind. People were always trying to make me vain about my hair and they admired this natural head ornament to such an extent that finally I decided to go to the hair dresser — to have it cut off. Why keep a useless ornament which only bothered me while running and jumping? The boys were much more comfortable. Why shouldn't I be like them? At first, the hair dresser was so shocked at my request that he stared at me and then burst out: "No, that would be too great a pity! I can't do it!"

"I'll simply go to someone else!" That helped. He first made a weak attempt to change my mind by pointing out that it would take my "magnificent hair" three whole years to reach its present fullness and length.

"That's exactly what I don't want. Why do you think I'm having it cut off?"

When he realized that I wouldn't be swayed, he took a deep breath and began cutting.

How dashing I felt when the deed was done! Just let someone dare insult me now by calling me "girl," like Winterfeld's Fritz did the other day! I was just as much a boy now as he. I was proud to look in the mirror now, something I usually had no time for.

"Would you like me to curl your hair with the curling iron?"

I broke into resounding laughter. "Oh God no! I don't want to turn myself into a dandy!"

The hair artist carefully wrapped my braid in silk paper and handed it to me solemnly.

"What should I do with it? *You* keep it."

"Would you sell it to me for 10 marks?"

I gladly accepted. I could buy a fine book with the money. And books always were and still are my passion. So I trotted home in high spirits where, naturally, a good licking was waiting for me. But who cared? One soon shakes that type of thing off, and nothing could change the fact that my hair was cut. Besides, I was considerably cheered up by my honestly earned money, with which I hurried to the book store on that very same day.

As already mentioned: I loved books passionately. However, I felt most drawn to the Robinsonades and the American Indian stories.. That's what I loved to talk about with my comrades. In fact, we not only talked about them, we also played cops and robbers and Indians. Our "cops and robbers" had gradually grown into a regular gang of robbers and finally gypsies. I was chosen leader, and a delicate, blond companion was the cook because he could fry sparrows so deliciously. The rest of us shot the sparrows with our sling shots. We had acquired a great knack and razzed each other when we missed.

In the midst of a field we had put up some tents and in one of them we had built a rock fireplace. The wood we stole — gypsies *have* to steal — from a neighboring construction site. By and by Wertenberg's Karl had dragged a frying pan, a box of matches, five dozen eggs, a big piece of bacon, butter and a bag of salt from his mother's kitchen. From the surrounding fields we gathered potatoes, turnips, etc., and so weren't at all deprived when we returned from hunting or other wild forays, for our famous cook had meanwhile prepared everything and even cleaned and plucked the sparrows.

But it all ended with a scare when we went to steal a chicken from a farmer in a distant village. The old guy didn't want to accept our explanation about our being gypsies; he agreed not to turn us over to the police only when we scraped together all our money and left it as a substitute for the loss he had almost suffered.

However, as captain of the gang I felt compelled to be harsh with the unworthy members who were stupid enough to let themselves get caught. At a sign from me, my comrades tied the culprits with string and handkerchiefs, which we usually had with us for the purpose of flying kites, and dragged them into the woods. I climbed a tree — I was a pro at it. Even if at that time the comfortable fashion of wearing a bicycle costume, i.e., tight-fitting plus-fours under the skirt, had unfortunately not yet been introduced, a very practical method of mine allowed me to keep up with the boys in all physical exercises, such as cartwheels, headstands, walking on hands, etc.: I always carried with me a large safety pin with which I fastened the back of my skirt (that I had pulled between my legs) to the front of my dress. This way I had the pants which were unfortunately denied me. I have to admit that I believed practically till I entered the university that the only difference between me and the boys consisted solely in dress and at times I was

27

very dissatisfied that from the beginning I had been stamped "girl" just because of my attire.

After I had taken my elevated seat from which I condemned the culprits, the fetters were untied at my commands, and I held strict judgment. The main culprits, i.e., the most stupid ones, received the crushing verdict to assist little Miss Hannchen — this was how we called our cook, whereas they called me by the name of "Hans" — with household chores, while the rest of us would embark chipper and gay on a warpath.

Silently, with brooding expressions, they accepted this cruelty because they knew quite well that refusal would only worsen their fate. They walked behind us just like in a funeral and followed us home, that is to say, into our tents. But when we had gotten undressed and Miss Hannchen asked one to scrape the carrots, the other to peel potatoes, indignation and revolt erupted.

"We're not girls, we can't and we won't cook!"

Hannchen tried to soothe both of them. In vain, Kurt grabbed a burning piece of kindling and lit the tent. Since other airy dwellings were not far off and a strong wind was blowing, the flames jumped merrily across and the fire flared up brightly. There could have been an accident; for, as I mentioned before, we were close to a big construction site with lots of wood. But the workers had immediately noticed the fire. They promptly rushed over, and within a short time managed to put it out.

Naturally, the story became known in town, and there was not one amongst our gang of gypsies who got away without a whipping. But what was worse yet: most of our pranks came to light. For example, it was told — not without some truth — that we had filched a pig in the neighboring village; after that, probably because we did not know how to slaughter it, fry it or make it into sausage, we supposedly put it into a pond. The animal swam happily to the opposite shore. There it was immediately picked up by a traveling merchant who happened to be passing by; he put it on his shoulder, probably with the intent of returning it to its owner. We considered the whole thing a fine sport, and we sent two delegates to the city hall in order to accuse the honest wanderer of pig theft. Anyway, the outcome was that the original owner got his little animal back.

For the sake of my comrades, I don't want to give away how much truth there is to the story; neither do I want to tell whether we really threw rocks through the windows of the church, as some insisted. It's enough that they thought us capable of doing so. Since this was "more than could be tolerated," each one of us was chastised severely, and I was forbidden once and for all to ever play with boys again.

Well, that wasn't so bad. I had played enough. The thought of compensating by associating with girls never occurred to me. Now my beloved books became my refuge. I went into my father's library and read everything I could get my hands on, especially war stories and sea adventures.

Why couldn't I become a soldier, why not a sailor? . . .

I don't want to imply that I loved studying. I mastered my lessons primarily because of ambition. Studying was easy for me. I just had to hear or read something once and I had it, and it even stayed in my head. Written assignments I practically shook out of my sleeve, so to speak. But even the once-over reading and the shaking-from-the-sleeve would have remained undone if I could have stood to be anything but the best student in the class.

In our little town we had a private school for boys. Since it had been established primarily for my cousins — my brothers were still too young at that time — I was permitted at the special request of my father to participate in all subjects. That was something for me! Naturally, this fortified me in my belief that "actually" I was a boy and not a girl.

Alsos I had sewing lessons, conversation in the newer languages, etc. Strangely enough, as fine a student as I was in the eyes of my male teachers, I was an insufferable, stubborn, willful student toward my female teachers — as long as I didn't have a crush on them. And I was swept into this emotion only by the twenty-year-old French woman because she had such wonderful large blue eyes, such magnificent black hair; because she was just simply beautiful. I soon found out that the officers of our little town shared my taste, which made me very proud. However, when one of them took the object of my adoration as his wife, I would have liked nothing better than to invite him to a duel. Nothing could make me go to the wedding celebrations to which I had been invited. I locked myself for half a day into my study and from time to time passionately stamped my foot. I was then fourteen.

The following month our instructions were to end. The boys, mostly older than I, had earned their primary certificate and went to a high school in some larger city. And what about me, who had passed with the highest grades? I was not accepted anywhere because I was — a girl. That was the first real disappointment of my life. Crying did not lie in my nature. I had to act, to defy. Just for spite I was going to pass my Abitur, and even sooner than my friends.

I got hold of the curriculum of the high school and studied it with my father's help. I also studied music; however, I never achieved perfection in this field.

One day I heard that the whole town was excited because a young society lady whom I knew quite well had passed her teacher's exam at the early age of eighteen. "If that's all!" I thought and went to the principal of the school from which she had graduated and had her test me privately. I was told that I had the necessary knowledge but not the prescribed age. I was too young even to be accepted into the advanced class. What to do now? Waiting was the answer. I had firmly resolved to pass this exam and nothing would change my mind.

With much trouble I convinced them to let me take, again privately and much sooner than my former playmates, the Abitur exam.

Now I was off to Switzerland in order to register at the university. At first I had to take philology. I had to pass my teachers' examination. After I had reached the prescribed age, I passed it brilliantly. When I took the exam, a professor told me that a girl who is even slightly gifted should not stop halfway; i.e., one also ought to take the administrator's exam.

Immediately I asked about prerequisites and, oh horror: found out that they consisted of five years practical teaching experience, two in a public school. Now what was I to do? But I soon made up my mind. I decided to say goodbye to my carefree student life, freedom and youthful madness. It meant first of all putting spectacles on my nose. However I decided since I'm not nearsighted to put some honorable wrinkles on my forehead instead and to blaze the way as a shining example for our younger generation on the path of virtue and science.

I was rather afraid of the restricted school life, but I didn't have to embark on it right away. During the first three years I could take the position of governess despite the fact that I was strongly advised against it. Nevertheless I listened to none of the remonstrances since I always followed my first inclinations and in this way experienced the truth of the saying: "The world belongs to the brave."

Again I was successful. I found an enviable position, had an above-average gifted student, very little work, an ideal family life and wonderful, delicious free time. This free time I used primarily to do some writing, which I had worked at ever since my twelfth year. Naturally, I had to tear myself away from it at times in order not to hurt the feelings of the beloved people with whom I lived by withdrawing completely from social functions. I went to dinners at the neighboring estates, to evening entertainments, even to balls. And since I was a cheerful, frolicsome creature — which I still am, by the way — I always amused myself royally, was welcome every place and had sufficient admirers.

"Ah hah!" one is going to say, "finally! It is too boring; nothing but: I did this and I did that, etc., etc. Not a thing about love?"

Patience! My so-called emotional life I have saved for the end. First the oats must be threshed completely, the pattern must be drawn to the end. It's not going to take much longer. I was very sad when the wonderful three years were over. I would have loved to have stayed longer with the people I had become so fond of. But how could I? Wasn't my stay with them only a means to an end? No, it was impossible. I resolutely resisted the begging, for I did not want to lose sight of my goal.

On with it then! Right into the real humdrum existence. I soon found a position as teacher, and I got used to my new profession more quickly than I had thought I would. Whenever I stood in front of the class, I became entirely the school teacher. I suppose I must have inherited this talent; whenever I left the students, who were attached to me with real enthusiasm, I became somebody entirely different.

Since I busily wrote during my free time, the two years had passed quite imperceptibly. I took the administrator's exam and — hurray; hurray! — back I went to the gay student life!

How did I spend my days as a student? Just like everyone else: One part of my activity consisted of loafing, drinking, gambling, drinking freedom in full draughts, climbing mountains, etc.! I am an enthusiastic nature lover, and a beautiful landscape can elate me to the point of intoxication, to the point of madness.

I generally grasp appealing new impressions with an inner fire, a passion, which makes a strange contrast to my outward coolness and calmness. One would think that something that is experienced in this manner could vanish quickly, would be blotted out quickly. No, it remains; that same fire of the greatest intensity keeps burning.

The second part of this university program, however, consisted of work. Besides astronomy and ancient languages, I had taken medicine as my major and, again, I did not want to lag behind my male colleagues in knowledge and skill. So I did rather well on my exam and settled down as free-lance science writer in one of the most idyllic areas of our fatherland, where, together with "her," I still lead a life which could not be more sublime or blissful if it were in Eden.

But you need to have courage, mind, courage. Take this courage, my sisters, and show that you have as much right to exist and to love as the "normal" world! Defy this world, and they will tolerate you, they will acknowledge you, and they will even envy you! Raise the weapons!

31

You must and you will succeed. I've done it. Why shouldn't you all, every single one of you, succeed?

"But," I hear the reply, "you are in Germany. Think of the Austrians! If you just had an idea of the tortures, the struggles, the fear of those who continually see the Damocles sword of the law suspended above them!" You poor unfortunates! When will the hour of deliverance come for you? When will it come for our brothers who share with us the fate of being exceptions to the average pattern, to the ancient, eternal natural law? But is it possible for Mother Nature to err? Can we even speak of exceptions, neurotic inclination, etc.? Is it not possible that we are an "intention" rather than an "accident?" All these questions have been and will be fought over innumerable times so that I don't want to enter into them at this point. Just throw me the gauntlet! I'll pick it up and you'll see I won't be reticent.

Raise the weapons! Until the tragic paragraph 175 is removed. How much misery it has already caused, how much suffering! Why should the innocent ones suffer, "in whom the heavens created feeling too?" But in a way, the average person does not want to understand. All right! I don't demand an exception to morality; what I demand is humanity, an impartiality, equal rights for all.

Finally, I promised to give a few glimpses of my love life. To make it short: I had never been in love and considered myself free of all "emotionalism," of all sensuality, until several years ago when I met the one woman who since then captures all my senses, to whom my life will be dedicated till my very last breath.

"No man's love must touch your heart with sinful flames of vain earthly lust," this is what I often thought when the big question confronted me: "Do you want to become mine? Do you want to follow me through life's storms?"

"No and no again!" I always said. Why? I didn't know myself. I felt a something which restrained me with magical force, and I'm very, very grateful to this "something." I laughed at love and thought the whole thing silly stuff, an invention of idle poets despite the fact that I wrote poems myself and had lost myself in this romantic subject at times.

Well, it was in its ugliest shape that love first approached me! He was married. I, barely fourteen, had been his student. My spirit, my quick grasp, my talents had dazzled him. During the private lesson he let his passion carry him away. In my consternation I ran away; however, I was so naive that I soon asked myself why I had fled and whether it wouldn't have been my duty to give him a kiss of gratitude?

To the master that I almost idolized. Fortunately he was honorable enough to have himself transferred immediately. The thought of what could have developed from the situation makes me shudder.

After that I had more or less acceptable offers. We contrasexuals are often surrounded by suitors and admirers. Whatever one can't get, entices. A fortress which does not give up till the hundredth skirmish has a hundredfold value.

And unfortunately, unfortunately most of us give in eventually. Almost all contrasexuals marry. You look at me baffled, and you possibly want to contradict me heatedly? You few unmarrieds who are aware — be careful! Watch out! I've warned you in time. Maybe you too will have a turn someday. But I fear less for you, you who are knowing, initiated and have your eyes wide open. I'm sure you are courageous enough to earn yourself that little bit of keep for which many thousands sell themselves. I'm also convinced that you won't be petty enough to let the pitiful ridicule attached to the concept "Spinster" make you throw yourselves under the yoke of marriage with a being whom you can't understand and love, who will want to assert his "he shall be your lord and master" from the first minute of your union.

Why is it that even in our enlightened age there should be a prejudice against the "spinster," a prejudice which causes much harm. One of the main reasons could be that, unfortunately, one is still to unfamiliar with the nature of contrasexuality, that one doesn't understand the marriages of those who are seemingly of the same sex. I was fortunate to run across various writings by Krafft-Ebing during my medical studies.

Oh, how I awoke! How my eyes were opened! How relieved, how determined about my goal I felt after reading this literature! I realized that I must never, never marry a man. I rendered account to myself about my life up until then, realized my complete coldness toward the opposite sex and admitted to myself that many a woman had because of her beauty, charm, gracefulness or natural intellect enchanted me even if she had not carried me away to the point of falling in love.

I wanted to remain watchful and keep my eyes open. The person who looks around attentively won't lose the way.

But oh! How many are still unconscious, not suspecting their true condition? It is those for whom I tremble. They choose amongst their many different suitors because of the above mentioned reasons or because of another, the one man who seems to them the most advantageous match; sometimes they even take the first acceptable one and entertain the gentle hope that "love comes with marriage." But, oh my!

I won't speak about the ensuing suffering, which I so often had the opportunity to observe. Of course there are those amongst us who possess sufficient imagination to dream themselves into the arms of the adored woman friend while lying in those of the man. In fact, an acquaintance confessed to me even that she became a mother in this way twice. Avoid such pretense, such hypocrisy, such deceit!

I continue to hesitate to talk about my marriage — this is what I deliberately call my relationship with my dear friend — because it seems so sacred to me; but it would be wrong to conceal something. I met "her" at a garden party. Nature had intoxicated me. I wanted to stretch out at the lakeshore in order to calm my excited inner self. There "she" lay underneath an oak tree, dressed entirely in pink.

No more! The whole thing was so fairytale fragrant, so dew fresh, that the story is like something out of a novel.

She was married. I went through all the storms of jealousy, of desperation, wanted to run away with her, to abduct her, and had to tell myself that I had no right. I found out after her husband's death, which happened suddenly, a hunting accident, that she was equally in love with me. From that moment on we have been living as a married couple. My lovely, dear wife bustles in our cozy home like a true German hausfrau, and I work and care for us both, as an active, vital husband.

from   OF THE NEW WOMAN AND HER LOVE:
        A BOOK FOR MATURE MINDS

by Elisabeth Dauthendey

(Berlin, Schuster & Loeffler, 1900)

Elisabeth Dauthendey's novel shows the confusion that was rampant during the turn of the century when "lesbianism" was widely viewed as a sexual act rather than a political choice. Her heroine is the New Woman, independent and spiritually realized — and too good for any of the men who are her contemporaries. Since men are not yet highly evolved, Dauthendey believes that women must find their happiness with like beings — i.e., other New Women. But they must not engage in "sapphic" practices, which are "impure" and "vulgar." However, they may lie together in bed, in each other's arms, and in "deep, blissful joy." Despite Dauthendey's Victorian prejudices about genital sex, she reveals her lesbian-feminist sentiments in her choice of a mate with whom she can live on equal terms and share every aspect of her life and work.

I

"It can no longer be denied. The new woman is here.
I am one myself and I want to tell you about her.
The new woman has arrived.
Centuries of suffering slowly brought her to maturity. It happened very gradually. Drop by drop she absorbed every conceivable pain into her psyche — she tolerated it, made it a part of her, and then suddenly felt that she could no longer bear it patiently, that her capacity for suffering would kill her if she did not finally want something else too, something stronger, healthier, more joyful than pain.

35

And slowly, in silence, this knowledge ripened like an exquisite fruit.

So quietly and demurely concealed — that when its rind finally burst open and the new and golden gleaming fruit shone on the tree of life — everyone stood before it in amazement.

Woman herself most of all.

For she now felt all eyes upon her. And first of all she had to get accustomed to it.

Now she had to tolerate scoffing surprise, stinging scorn, brutal doubt — all this had to be added to her suffering in order to free her fully and finally from the old pain, to make her victorious.

But now she has freed herself, and with a shudder she looks down from her new height into the narrowness and darkness she left and onto those thousands who still move within that realm, contented and dull — but what can a blind person know of darkness and a lame one of dancing feet?

The new woman is a million miles ahead of those of her sex who remained behind. They see with different eyes and therefore they no longer find their way to each other; they speak a different language and therefore they no longer understand each other.

The purely erotic element of woman, out of which Christianity made woman's demon, has risen from the dark, chaotic realm of the senses to a lighter, freer height of will.

From the mysterious, undifferentiating drive toward man, which usually meant merely more darkness added to all the other gloom of her narrow existence — a discriminating, combative will has emerged which permits her to choose only that special man who is an answer and a strength and a deliverance to her psyche which desires light.

This new — this Athenian element in woman: her delight in herself and the freedom of her nature, this wanting to remain in control of the treasures of her soul and body — this is what puts the woman of today into a dangerous position in relation to the woman of yesterday and the man who still lives in the dark ages.

And so she is living in noon brightness with her new vision and noon heat with her new will. She knows her past and hates it and does not want it back for anything.

She knows what her present means and she suffers, but with new, magnificent pain which contains a thousand seeds of blissful joy for her daughters and her daughters' daughters.

She intimates their future, the great future of new-found beauty, and a gentle reflection of bliss shines in her own soul, and she bears her suffering.

And in this knowledge of ourselves, our suffering, the growth of our personality, lie our pains and our raptures. For the woman of today knows that she is condemned to loneliness. That she will never know the final completion of her being in the giving and receiving of love from the man of her choice.

Because this man does not yet exist. And she cannot love indiscriminately — she cannot accept sex which is ruled merely by sex.

Her intellect has awakened. After her eternally long sleep and her sleep-walking she has finally been incarnated in her highest form. But be not afraid. We will never be "des êtres simplement raisonables."

Never.

The deepest roots of our being rest too firmly in the dark, sacred, motherly depth of the mysterious vital warmth which nourishes us all.

For us, whose organism connects us so closely with the eternally fruitful, the eternally giving mother's womb of earth — giving remains the highest pleasure — and giving for us comes from the heart and not from the intellect.

Only we no longer do this indiscriminately.

We want to know our beloved. It is not enough that he be merely a man.

The human in man, his personality — the last — the best — the finest in him — this is what we want from him.

But he first must attain this excellence. And the man of today does not yet have it. He still dwells with the woman of yesterday and for the time being feels most comfortable with her. The new woman now has to form him for herself — has to form him in her thoughts.

She has to transport the burning wishes of her soul into his being and she has to want him this way and no other way — until he is here — born from the motherly, warm womb of her woman's will as she envisions him — and for him the new young mother-women long. As the Messiah was born out of the long hope of his people.

But the new woman is destined to remain lonely if the new man doesn't arrive soon.

She knows about this loneliness and she takes it upon herself like a heroine; she is conscious of the reasons for forgoing the greatest happiness of a short blissful life — for the time being this is the only painful reward for her quiet, long, difficult struggle toward a new life — for, as Maeterlinck, the profound psychologist says:

"On ne choisit pas ses raisons, on les mérite comme des récompenses."

II

But why do our men have this deathly fear of and defense against women's progress?

This being horrified, cursing, ranting and raving in order to dumbfound, to hold women back, to make them unsure — is it perhaps the impotent rage of a god who sees his believers desert him — the fear of empty temples, of feet which no longer want to kneel, voices which no longer tremble in adoration; eyes which have learned to look behind the incense — the great torment and the stony horror of the Götterdämmerung in the kingdom of those who up until now had let themselves be worshipped and who no longer can do without the bliss of this prostrate, kneeling love — as much as they may ridicule it and mock it and step on it?

But why this fear? Does not each dawn bring a new light? Look at the red golden sun which rises for you above the low-hanging clouds of the maiden's humility in the strong, fresh love of the newly created woman.

But until man's eyes have become strong enough for the new sunrise — must I suffer?

If I cannot drink from the best cup, should I renounce all wine?

You can see that I esteem the pleasure of love as the highest good — that I do not despise man and what he can add to woman's life.

But I want to drink the precious potion unadulterated from golden bowls. Where is the man who would quench my thirst with this intoxication and this comfort?

He does not exist."

The narrator tells us that her parents had a very traditional marriage. Her father was a cold, stern man, unable to express feelings or affection. Her mother loved her husband despite the fact that she could not share her feelings with him. Lenore learns through her mother's journal that she killed herself because of insufferable loneliness. After the mother's death father and daughter live together for several years. The stern father gradually goes blind and mellows. His relationship with his daughter becomes quite close and warm before he dies. Lenore then spends several years alone.

After some time has passed, she receives a call from a friend who is staying at a sanatorium with her daughter. Lenore goes to visit her. The friend is trying to recuperate from the effects of a disastrous marriage. However, the exhaustion is too far advanced and she does not get well. Before she dies, she makes Lenore promise to take care of her daughter, Yvette.

The director of the sanatorium, a mercurial, ingenious man, persuades Lenore to stay on for a while. She experiences a brief infatuation for him, and then disillusionment sets in: the director is merely another ruthless male out to appease his debased appetites.

Lenore has noticed one of the patients, a gentle man whose past dissolute life has caused him to be paralyzed from the waist down. He had spent his life lusting after, and sexually exploiting women, but the suffering he experienced because of his ensuing paralysis made him see women in another light. Through suffering, he has acquired a beautiful, perfect soul. Lenore falls in love with the sensitive cripple and resolves to take care of him. She takes him and her friend's sixteen-year-old daughter, Yvette, home.

For some time, the three lead peaceful lives. Lenore muses about the man who was not her husband, the child who was not her child and herself who stands between them "with a powerful woman's love for a man and a sacred tenderness for a child."

Lenore is happy. Only at night is she tortured with abysmal pain. There is, after all, no possibility of sexual gratification with her paralyzed beloved.

Yvette remembers her mother, who had rarely paid much attention to her. Whenever she talked about her mother:

"Her voice was strangely bitter.

The outline of her slender and tall frame was austere.

She looked like a flower which had been stylized by a master's hand.

Hair and eyes dark and heavy. The mouth chaste and warm like a sun-ripe fruit of the South.

Her hands were innocent like flowers from paradise, but her manner of seizing things was solid and desiring.

That's how Yvette was."

Yvette, too, loves the paralyzed companion. Chastely, of course. When he dies, their love for him binds the two women even closer to each other.

As time goes by, Yvette's body matures. It is no longer severe but is pleasingly rounded. She detests society. Lenore lets her engage in sports instead. After some time, she takes Yvette south and tells her to go out into the world for three years. There is to be no communication between them. Their separation causes terrible pain on both sides.

Lenore wonders what to do. Should she give up looking for happiness altogether? No, she decides. She is too full of life yet. Instead of waiting for the man, or the child, she will hope for the *woman, an ersatz person with whom to share love and loneliness.*

Lenore thinks:

"With what joyfulness will we greet each other — you and I.

Our handshake will be the symbol of a secret brotherhood (*sic.*)."

She goes farther south and settles down in a boarding house. At first she concentrates on working and writes her autobiography for those "who are quietly progressing toward a new age." *In between work she keeps looking for the perfect woman. Finally:*

"I immediately noticed her when I found her sitting opposite me at the dinner table for the first time.

The dark eyes were like a pair of suns in the pale, cool face. The large mouth and the strong chin had powerful, energetic lines which could almost seem brutal — however, under those soft, glowing eyes they imparted the impression of a quiet, self-assured feeling of power. The short dark hair fell in soft waves around the beautiful, distinctly cut face. Her hands were very white, but thickset and heavy, and did not match the perfect, clear shape of her head. If you had seen them by themselves, you would have thought them strange; but this way the face, particularly those radiant, enticing, victorious eyes, made you forget them.

Our glances met often.

She looked at me long and inquiringly, for she, too, found in me something different, something not commonplace.

Rasti Tabera had Spanish blood in her veins, but for many decades it had been mixed with German blood, and this accounted for her double nature, cool thoughtfulness and burning impulsiveness, which was evident in her beautiful pale face.

She was the owner of a large bank in northern Germany, had overworked herself and had come to this place to rest.

This will toward heavy work alone differentiated her from the majority of women. We became closer. Slowly and irresistibly we were drawn to each other.

Then, after the first shyness had been conquered, we were together daily.

We took long hikes on mountains and in valleys.

And the seductive air of the South drew our souls faster and more gently into that total intimacy after which there remains only one fine veil between the you and the I — hiding the last enticing secret which leads us to an abyss or to a heaven.

I found out about her hard youth from which she struggled with an iron will to reach a secure position in life. I knew about all the brutality and meanness from both man and woman that she had experienced on her journey. Especially from man, since she moved in his tracks and since she won her security in his havens.

40

And I knew about man's ruthless courtship when she had reached her goal and had, despite all, become an object of value in the market.

I understood her disgust for man.

'Man is something which must be overcome' – this is how she transposed Nietzsche's expression into the key of her own mood.

'How do you overcome him in yourself? With work?'

She laughed. A somewhat hard, mocking laugh which reminded me of the vibration of a broken string.

'Work has never been more than a means to an end for me.'

'And what is your end?'

'Pleasure.'

'In what?'

'In all good and beautiful things in life.'

'Then you are a materialist?'

'But certainly – what else could one be at the present time?'

'Many things. But this does not bother me as far as you are concerned. I love an honest acknowledgment of our attitudes toward life and all honest action. In the last analysis, everyone is oriented toward pleasure and it is only a question of – at which level do we find it and look for it.'

And since I always saw her honestly enjoying her days in quiet happiness and with all the attractive things around her – as though she were resting in satisfied memories and collecting herself for new joys – I did not resist her approach which became warmer and warmer, hoping finally to find the deepest, most valuable part of her being.

I yielded to her wish and moved with her into a small villa which stood in the midst of the rich fragrance of Riviera roses.

In our daily togetherness, I always delighted anew in her beauty. The fullness of her form gave her movements a lazy, slow quality compared to which her lightning-like mind seemed strangely incongruous; she should have thought in a dreamy, slow way, as beautiful Creoles do.

A few weeks passed quickly for us, both of us at work.

She had to take care of a lot of business even from where we were staying.

But still I did not know her completely; still a last reserve lay over her being; there was something that wanted to reach me but did not find the way; something which felt for my soul with gentle groping – this is what I often sensed emanating from her and going back to her, and then the look of her sun-hot, enticing eyes was puzzling to me.

41

But finally came the hour of total recognition.

It was during a night in February.

Our balcony doors were wide open. The large impetuous sound of the ocean surged upward, the sky could barely carry the golden splendor of the stars and the air vibrated with sultry waves of fragrance from the earth. The beauty of the night kept me from sleeping.

I stepped out onto the balcony and let the mysterious spell of this fruitful terrestrial magnificence put me into a happy dream state.

Suddenly Rasti was beside me. I had not heard her coming; she had come, like I, on naked soles out into the balmy night.

'You too can't sleep,' she said. 'I was lying there and was longing for you as I've been longing for weeks — don't you feel it, you beautiful, magnificent woman.'

And she put her arms around my neck heavily.

Then she fell down before me, kissed my feet, clasped my knees.

'Be mine, wholly mine, in boundless tenderness — this is how I want to enjoy you.'

And before I could recover from my astonishment, she had picked me up in her strong arms and carried me over the threshold of the room onto my bed.

She fell upon me with vehement, frantic caresses which I could not immediately ward off since I was so utterly unprepared.

Finally, however, I succeeded in freeing myself from her.

Firmly but gently I took her into my arms — because I felt sorry for her — and led her back into her room and closed the door between us.

Then she understood me and realized that it was not Sapphic love that I wanted, that my womanly instincts were too complete and too healthy.

And our paths separated."

Lenore goes her lonely way again. She publishes her autobiography. Many women write. Some misunderstand her. One, especially, is eager to share her life with her, but again she becomes disgusted about the other's "impure motives" *and shakes her off. She now finds that she is exhausted.* "Nothing troubles the soul more deeply than when its best and finest aspects are judged as impure and vulgar.

Then, in the midst of my misery came a letter from Yvette:

'I am waiting for you, beloved — I am at home, punctually to the day and hour of your wish. Come soon.'

I hurried home full of new hope and new fear: would I find her my own — just as I had carried her picture in my heart; would she have completely fulfilled the promise of her being; would she have grown into that type of beauty of which Zarathustra says, '— pure and fine, resembling a precious stone, illuminated by the virtues of a world which does not yet exist.'

VIII

It was blooming May when we were reunited at the threshold of my house.

Without a sound, in the silent ardor of deep, blissful joy we lay in each other's arms.

And the breath of our beating pulses was just enough to let us speak the beloved name —

'Lenore —'

'Yvette.'

She led me into my room, which was full of the young, green, astringent fragrance of spring.

In the middle of the room was an easel, with a small rectangular picture on it which contained nothing but two human hands that hold each other tight and warm as if for all eternity.

I stepped closer. It was not difficult to recognize my own hand in that which had been painted full-size; and hers was the other one, of which could be seen only the thumb and the enclosing fingertips, painted so delicately and surely — Yvette's slender, flexible fingers with the clear oval of the nails — and the two hands ardently grasped each other, and the fingers dug deep into the soft flesh of one another.

One felt the current of love which held these hands together.

We exchanged looks in front of this painting, and we understood each other.

'But you were searching for happiness, my Yvette, weren't you?'

'Yes, I always heard your encouraging words in my ears and searched for it — but — they all had so much clay on their hands and no sky in their hearts — once — But I'll tell you another time; today I want to be happy — happy — happy that I have you back.'

'And this has become your work now?'

'Yes — I tried all kinds of things — but this is what appeals to my heart.'

'And you were very diligent and faithful, I can tell from this painting.'

'You know that whatever I love, I love wholly and faithfully.'

'But that I should have you again — you — you my only love!'

'I think you'll be satisfied with me, for I have lived as if your soul were walking beside me — your beautiful, rich, strong soul, which I always felt at the roots of my being like strength-giving mother earth — oh, to think that I have you back again!'

With sacred delight I let this warm gush of love engulf my heart.

The blooming young woman in the fullness of her beauty and the mature woman in the fullness of her experience and her immortal hope for the coming life: these two with strong faith in each other, in pure knowledge of each other — united in that devotion with which only women can love; was that not the ultimate happiness which life owed me and which I had gone out into the world to find?

I accepted it as the precious gift of fate. Over our life came the blissful peace of satisfied longing.

Like precious jewelry our love permeated our everyday life and gilded it, as the radiant sun dips everything it touches into gold and fire and beauty.

Our quiet, happy home now was full of eager work — it was also full of struggle and worry about our growth in our work; but deep within us there was peace and beauty and purity — and the richness and the profound joy of love with waits an eternity.

This is how we lived together through delightful times.

Yvette and I.

Each understood the other's work, savored the most hidden treasures of the other's soul in the manifestations of her art, and our days passed for us like the gently rippling waves of the ocean when it seems to rest under the golden sun and the blue of the sky and yet its depths are in eternal movement.

I had a studio furnished for Yvette beside my study. There she created her marvelous works of art.

One could call her the painter of longing. Her paintings were of the suffering of our times, and they were so intensely moving that they were almost painful to see — this noble suffering, which is experienced only by the best who struggle in the front lines of progressive, evolving humanity.

One of those pictures I cannot forget.

She called it Mother's Happiness.

But how new this ancient tale became under her hand.

A woman, almost life size, painted only to her knees, leaned against the whitish wall of a house of which one could see only one protruding corner — a trellis with young vine leaves stretched above her.

The child lay on her breast. There was nothing in her face of the usual expression of pride about her maternal achievement, that satisfied smile of complete fulfillment in which one could see an

44

individual with hope and promise dissolve instead into a stupid nothing.

Here the mother holds the child with her strong hands, tightly and warmly, against her nourishing breast — but she gazes seriously and nobly with undeniable longing into the immeasurable distances as if to stretch her soul toward the furthest and the highest so that she may grow with that which grew from her, in order to remain above it, in order to prepare its path toward growth in its own turn.

How tenderly she who created such works must have felt about motherhood; she had been wholly created for it with her blooming body and her ardent soul.

And to such a woman the garden of marriage was to be closed!

I felt as if I should have called to the world in a loud voice:

'You men who are already capable of great, rare love, make women like these mothers! Make her mother, the woman of today, so that she may implant her new nature into a new generation which will then be capable of the shining happiness of the best.

But in order to achieve this, you both must want something new — not only must the woman want to reach the ultimate height in complete purity and self-sacrifice — but the man, too, must have become wholly united with her in this desire for purity and the heights.

For how should your sex be capable of elevating itself if the desire of its fathers does not elevate itself?'

'You don't hate man, do you,' I asked Yvette, 'since you keep so adamantly silent in regard to him?'

'How could I — since he means woman's salvation; he helps her achieve her ultimate, deepest, holiest beauty? And to feel that we won't experience this completion means such a bitter, bitter pain.'

How powerful must be that which now repels us in man that we would rather bear this pain than accept his love?

'Look,' she said and looked out onto the highway on which the Sunday crowds swarmed out into field and forest.

'Look at this threefold foolishness of father, mother and child — would you like to see me impoverished like that?'

'Not like this — more beautiful — differently.'

'How can it be different as long as man thinks of us in such a lowly manner that he feels justified in taking all from one part of our sex — in order then to despise woman for it — and in daring to offer the other part his used-up, dirty life instead of all of its untouched fullness of being.'

45

She had tears in her eyes.

I embraced her with warmth and firmness.

'How lucky for us that we don't have to remain lonely and completely without happiness.'

So my life had finally achieved its ultimate harmony — that gentle, peaceful equilibrium between wanting and having which the mature person creates for herself in order not to feel her life to be a burden.

We had found the solution for the famishing woman of today, whose life is condemned to the severest privations because her new self cannot tolerate the love of man as he is.

Just as man cannot live for bread alone, so woman's soul cannot find complete satisfaction in work.

For a time she believed she could lose herself wholly in work. The first draught from these springs which were new to her intoxicated her and made her forget her suffering, her want, but soon she realized that work was salvation for her only for a time — sometimes for a long time — but this one-sided pursuit cut off the arteries of her being, it blocked something in her which she felt was her very own, her most precious and which she could not give up without losing faith in herself.

This finest, tenderest, most sacred warmth of her inner self needed a gentle, nurturing, dependable presence if it was not to perish for lack of nourishment.

And who could give all this to her better than a being of her own kind who is suffering from the same affliction and is also looking for an accepting, grateful soul on which to bestow her love.

This is why the new woman must look for friendship with woman as ardently as the future man will look for love with woman.

And the peaceful happiness that woman will find in woman will awaken men and force them to question and wonder, and this will bring the sexes closer to each other.

'They are happy without us.'

'What are they giving each other?'

'Why don't they want us anymore?' or —

'Do they need something other than what we've been giving them all along?' — this is what the best amongst men will ask if more and more of the best women will resist marriage as it is now.

And as soon as there is this questioning, they'll understand the answer.

Yes, we want you to be different.

We want you to have more depth, more warmth, more sympathy if

46

you are to relate to us. Most of all we want you pure in love, just as you have for centuries demanded of us the utmost purity.

Our sex no longer wants to be measured by a double standard.

Already dawn is breaking in gentle, light waves through darkness; everywhere the realization stirs amongst a few — for the time being — but amongst the best of men, that relationships will have to change between the sexes.

Wherever minds are opening in this evolving, changing way, we send our joyful wishes and let our hearts tremble with blissful rapture for those who come after us and who will finally reap this happiness worthy of humans.

We, however, who are too early and whose time has not yet come, will be satisfied with the joy of the prophets whose life-long hope has made their eyes and ears acute enough to see and to hear the future and who call to the waiting with the voice of promise: 'The enormous event is already taking place and is spreading; it has not yet reached the ears of all humans. Lightning and thunder need time, the light of the stars needs time — actions need time, even after they have happened, before they are seen and heard.'

Look, it is coming — it is close, the great noon of the New Happiness which will speak thusly:

'Marriage: that is what I call the wish of two people to create something which is more than those who created it.'

You are not just to create *forth*, to procreate, but to create *up* and toward perfection:

The garden of marriage may help you to do so!"

from   **AS I SEE IT**

by Mrs. M. F.

(from *Yearbook of Intermediate Sexual Types*,
Volume III, Leipzig, 1901)

By 1901 lesbianism, as the sexologists defined it, became a not infrequent theme in popular literature. The anonymous author of this essay happens on a book whose title is revealing enough of its contents, The Disinherited of Love's Happiness. *Learning from the book that her kind end in "madness or suicide," she convinces herself that she must sublimate the affections she has had since girlhood and become instead a "spiritual" person. We may believe that many lesbians of her generation, who — like most Victorian women — were brought up to believe that sex was a sin, found similar "solutions."*

Be Strong — Cast your message
into the world!

In school all the girls had a crush on the male teacher of literature — not I. The French teacher was the one who made my heart beat faster. Her contract was for only one year. During this time I attacked French with fiery zeal. When she left town, I felt so pitiful and miserable that I didn't know what to do with myself. Then, for a long time nothing happened. I grew — that was all. Again, another woman teacher brought me to life. This time it was an English woman who had come into our house. I was about fourteen years old. Miss Mary awakened all the soft, tender impulses of my heart. There was no student more willing, none more eager, none who progressed more quickly than I. Soon I lived only for this blonde stranger who was still young herself and who was likewise inclined toward me in the warmest, nicest way. We read Elise Polke's "Musical Fairytales," and the sky was full of violins for us. After two years we were parted.

I believe that the capacity for suffering in a child is generally underestimated. If I look back now on how I raced through the woods, I feel a virtual compassion for the poor little girl whose quivering heart drove her into misery and desperation.

Again nothing happened for a while. My so-called "admirers" seemed only silly to me. Then I married when I was seventeen. I think men found me a darling little thing whom one could easily like. Since I had a lot of brothers and sisters, and there was hardly any talk about "careers" for girls at that time, my parents thought it best to "get rid of them" as soon as possible. Despite all parental love, each girl who was unmarried meant one mouth more to feed. Even though my bridegroom turned out not to be tender, I wasn't especially unhappy, since my marriage meant to me a possible bridge toward a reunion with Miss Mary. This thought made everything appear sweet to me. As far as I can remember, my emotional development did not undergo great changes at that time. I still had not become my own self, but I didn't suffer in that role that had been imposed on me. I was wife and mother and − nothing − despite all.

I had not seen the English woman for years when I met an Austrian woman, a person who was in all respects my complete opposite. Everything separated us: she was strength, I softness; she inconsiderate to the point of brutality when it meant achieving what she wanted, I weak to the point of cowardice in the same situation. Nothing seemed to unite us: she the descendant of the bluest blood, I Jewish. Nevertheless, from the beginning there was something stronger than all barriers. We met on a purely spiritual level, and we became a necessity for each other. I did not know that a passionate friendship could have such decisive impact on my life.

We were together for only a few weeks; then we had a correspondence which, for years, left nothing to be desired in uniqueness. The pen of my friend brought to me everything that happened in the realm of literature, politics, art and science. Outbursts of tenderness hardly occurred on her side. "You are there and you are my creature," seemed to her so self-evident that she never questioned it. What I had to tell her was always wrapped in a mantle of tender devotion. At first I often did not know what to write. But by and by my spirit gained strength, my soul wings, I stood up tall, a new world began to glimmer before my eyes. Years came and went. Art united us with a strong bond; I was always ready to experience with her the impulse of her artist's soul, to take upon me her suffering, to triumph in her success. And so, what had at first been vicarious experiencing, gained life of its own. Seeds which had been lying fallow within me began to sprout forcefully. She taught me joys and sufferings.

It was strange that my friend's presence never brought me pure sunshine. Quite the contrary. Despite the joy of knowing her in my proximity for a few days or weeks, my nerves would quiver in an incomprehensible rebellion — either I cried or I was seized by an exuberant hilarity. I could not master these mysterious moods. Only when I was separated from her would my strength return.

Once, when we parted after having been together for a short while, I ambled through the streets of Leipzig, since my train was not due for some time. Our goodbye made my limbs feel dull and leaden; at the same time I felt dissatisfied — empty — lonely. I stopped in front of a bookstore. My eyes scanned the book titles. *The Disinherited of Love's Happiness,* what was that? Magnetically the words whose meaning was an utter mystery to me attracted me. Slowly it began to dawn in me that I, especially I, ought to be interested in this book. Ought I to buy it? I was torn. Actually, I felt a horror of the unknown content, and yet — and yet — I held it in my hands tremblingly — tremblingly, as if my death sentence were to be pronounced. I hurried to the train; then I perused the pages — and I tore them in half and threw them out the window. I would have liked to have jumped after them. A confused, tangled picture had slid into my soul — remembered something about "ending in madness or suicide." I was thirty-two at that time. The leave-taking, the summer's heat were already tormenting my nerves — this combined with the impressions of the book threw me onto a sickbed. To die after that revelation — this seemed to me the only hope, the only solution. Yes, I wanted to die — but — I did not die. I continued to be shaken by confused terror to which my reason could easily have fallen victim. Nevertheless I recuperated. The book, which was so unlike my daily life, disappeared from my memory like a dark dream. At first I had attempted to give up my friend, but when I wrote her (who did not suspect the connection) something about "to put a stop to it and to end it," she simply laughed at me. So everything remained the same. Soon after that she became infatuated with a man. I suffered all the torments of jealousy although I was convinced that no one could match the intensity of my feeling, that nobody could follow the flights of her spirit as I could. Quietly, slowly, a change occurred within me. Fully and wholly I experienced the saying: "I searched for you and found myself." Myself — myself — filled with timorous wondering; numbly, I sensed my kingdom. Everything had opened, every grain of seed which had sprung from her influence, was bearing fruit. And blissfully I stretched my limbs. No more torturous shivers of fear and pain. My innermost inclination toward woman, toward beings of my own sex, which determined everything that life had destined for me in terms of becoming and growth, no longer frightened me. I was overcome by an almost blissful certainty: I could distinguish so much spiritual nobility and purity in my feelings that I looked smilingly on all the slime and dirt which life has in store almost everywhere.

I have not lost any of life's values. On the contrary, spiritual people offer me a many-faceted spiritual sympathy, rich in nuances. Unconsciously, I taught many that loving a soul is deep magic. My friends need me. I share their interests; and we have beautiful role-free relationships. Yes, my nature elicits apparently quite often in man the wonderful nuance of sympathetic feelings which the French so excellently call "l'amitié amoureuse"; a special melody vibrates between us. And a special melody resounds in the stillness of my soul: all the fine, tender sensations which my friend has given me condense themselves for me into creative energy — the ecstasies of my heart take on form and shape; out of the spiritualization of my instincts a silvery pure spring flows for me, gushes passion and fervor; my exceptional soul lifts me upward above suffering and torment; this is how a talent has been generated and has come to life.

from   **A GIRL FROM A NICE FAMILY:**
THE HISTORY OF A YOUNG GIRL'S SUFFERING

by Gabriele Reuter

(Berlin, 1895)

*This excerpt from Gabriele Reuter's novel contains a scene which
was almost requisite in nineteenth-century novels about girls — a
boarding-school love affair. In 1895 such a relationship, which may
have been fraught with adolescent turmoil, was still, nevertheless, not
considered "abnormal." Only with the increasing popular spread of the
sexologists' theories did it come to be widely believed that love between
young girls leads to love between women, which is "sick."*

A Girl From a Nice Family *traces the life of Agathe Heidling from
childhood to middle-aged spinsterhood. Her entire education is directed
toward one goal: to mold her into the perfect wife. She is unassuming,
nurturing, frugal, unobtrusively intelligent, extremely well-mannered and a
marvelous housekeeper. Yet she never manages to catch a suitable
husband. At novel's end, having forfeited the fulfillment of wife- and
mother-hood, she has turned into a pitiable, peaked-faced spinster,
dependent on the generosity of her brother.*

*At the end of the novel, her brother's wife Eugenie, Agathe's opposite
in every respect, has become one of her most trying adversaries. Ironically,
it is Eugenie who had been Agathe's closest friend during her early life
and with whom she had been involved in an intense girlhood crush while
both attended boarding school.*

"Agathe lived in the same dormitory with Eugenie. At first, she
suffered from the childish fear that Eugenie would make some sort of
allusions to the talks they had engaged in as little girls. But Eugenie
seemed to have forgotten about them altogether. She had turned into

53

a pretty, already quite elegant young girl. Much to her own amazement, Agathe immediately was seized with a passionate love for her. She now could think of no greater pleasure than to be with Eugenie Wintrow, to snuggle up to her and to kiss her. Eugenie treated her childhood friend's attachment like the adoration of a man. At times she was cold and hard and harshly rejected Agathe's caresses. Agathe could not soften her through the offer to solve her math problems nor through adoring letters which she placed on her friend's pillow. Suddenly, however, Eugenie would once again be charmingly sweet.

Lately Agathe was suffering from toothaches and swollen cheeks. When she lay moaning and groaning on her bed behind the screen — the dormitory was separated in this way into different little private spaces — Eugenie came sneaking over to her on her bare feet, brought eau de cologne or chloroform, and sat at her bed and stroked her forehead slowly and rhythmically until the pain subsided and Agathe fell asleep under the magical effect of the soft girl's hand.

Eugenie had a practical nature; without much deliberation, she perceived in each situation what was to be done. She was very popular amongst the other adolescent girls. Agathe was often tortured by jealousy when Eugenie walked with others or if, at times, she even put her arm around the waist of another girl."

Agathe's jealousy is heightened when Eugenie takes a liking to Klotilde, a new student.

"Right away, on the first evening, Eugenie walked on the grounds with the new girl and let herself be instructed on how to make up her nose Greek fashion. Agathe dared to make a timid objection. However, she fared badly. During the next few days Eugenie neglected her in a truly brutal way. A violent correspondence ensued between the two dormitory companions. In purple prose they wrote each other the most insulting things. Agathe cried away entire nights in rage and jealousy. Finally, Eugenie flat out declared that she was in love with Klotilde; she had felt it from the first moment. You could not fight love, and Agathe should look for another friend. They no longer spoke to each other. They passed each other without a glance."

from   **FROM CHILDHOOD TO MATURITY**

by Gabriele Reuter

(Berlin, S. Fischer, 1921)

This excerpt from Gabriele Reuter's autobiographical novel shows the depth of passion one female might experience for another without acknowledging that it is "lesbian." While Gabriele believes that she can best interest Elizabeth in her by discussing what is commonly acknowledged — a heterosexual passion — her involvement with males is limited to her imagination or to the ethereal. Gabriele never tells Elizabeth about her real passion for her, since she has no words for it, "lesbian" not being applicable because it meant a congenital deformity or a sexual act. Reuter shows how on a personal level heterosexuality is encouraged while love between women is relegated to the realm of the unspoken, and thus can come to nothing.

The narrator, Gabriele, reminisces about her childhood. She remembers a scene in which she overheard her two aunts talk about her, one of them remarking that Gabriele might be an exceedingly quiet child, but that she certainly was not stupid. Her aunt Elizabeth concluded the discussion with the observation: "Oh well, if one's as pretty as Ella, one could even afford to be a little stupid!"

From this moment on Gabriele desires only intelligence and wit in order to impress the adored aunt, to win her affection. But she is utterly tongue-tied in her presence. At one point she observes:

"When I saw the young woman with the child at her breast, wearing a rapt expression, with her slender, pale hands like a madonna, when I saw her thus sitting in the grape arbor with the green shadows and the golden lights dancing around her, my heart was torn. I could have burst into tears and yet I was so full of bliss. To kneel silently by her

55

side, not saying a word — only gazing at her: that pale, freckled slender face with the tragic mouth, the deeply soulful eyes and the dark hair which forever hung over her forehead in wild strands and never wanted to settle into the chaste coiffure its owner tried to achieve — this unseemly, so incredibly lively head on the magnificently shaped body whose movements were always full of complete harmony and beauty.

But for heaven's sake, one had to be careful. Not a sentimental word, no adoring glance! In the mantle of this rapt madonna lurked an unquenchable fondness for ridicule and an earthy sense of humor with a gift for grotesque comparisons — characteristics so rare in a woman. . . . Despite her aristocratic deportment Elizabeth had nothing in common with the typical modern lady. I always thought: this is how Renaissance women must have been according to the pictures artists and poets have handed down to us: a woman full of lust for power — despite great depth of soul and the wealth of a playful mind not without harshness and cruelty. Oh yes — she was capable of enjoying cruelty, this wife and loving mother — and it intrigued her to see young people tremble because of her proximity."

One day Gabriele's family goes on a picnic together with Elizabeth: "Everything took place according to our program, and there would be nothing noteworthy about this day. However, on this hot afternoon in the sun-dried firwoods, a moment occurred which was to be a deciding factor in the mental and psychic development of my youth. Like most such decisions it seemed harmless and almost trivial. Elizabeth asked me to accompany her from our picnic spot out into the woods, she had to redo her braids. The heavy fake braids, which women were in the habit of wearing and with which one tried to achieve a dignified and house-wifely impression, kept falling out of her own thin willful hair nearly hourly; this did not bother her at all. When they suddenly slid down her back like live slippery animals or fell over her shoulders, they were simply put up again, which certainly did not contribute to the neatness of her hairdo. And this is how I still see her, standing under the pitch-fragrant fir trees, her braid in her hand, suddenly asking me unexpectedly whether I did not carry an unhappy love in my heart. I should go ahead and open myself up to her, she had great empathy for young girls, many had already confessed to her. Even if she could do nothing for me, simply talking about such things meant a great relief and, at times, a healing. For she had to tell me this: there was something morbid about me. At first she had thought I was merely stupid. But now she had observed me for some time and discovered that I was not stupid at all. So some other reason had to lie at the

56

bottom of my stubborn reserve and taciturnity, and she was going to find me out!

I stood crimson with shame before these penetrating questions while Elizabeth's beautiful, pale hands raked her unruly hair and with a kind of fury stuck countless pins into it every which way.

What could I say? I would have liked to have thrown myself at her bosom to have a good cry, but she did not care for caresses — a kiss on the hand while saying goodnight was all she permitted now and then.

I did have a secret. In my dreams I had been living and weaving it for months. But how could I have put it into words? And especially before this woman I worshipped so deeply, whose superior smile made me desperate? And wouldn't anyone reasonable and sober laugh? Two forces were violently struggling within me. The longing to get closer to her who had asked me to confide in her by making my confession, a need to abase myself before her by opening to her my silly, fantasy-filled heart, and the strong insinuation that all the rapture of my dreams might be destroyed if I tried to clothe the unspeakable in words and to submit to human judgment.

"Of course it's one of the cousins from Althaldensleben?" she inquired, mentioning first this and then that name.

"Oh — that's long past," I exclaimed, fighting with tears. No, it was impossible! How could I admit to Elizabeth that I was in love with a painting — a painting of a young, beautiful prince, which, in fact, was really nothing but a picture to me, for other photographs or busts of this very same prince did not have that wonderful effect on me; they left me unmoved and disappointed until I revived my intoxicated feeling of joy and suffering by imagining myself in all kinds of romantic dream adventures with the figure in the painting. The uneventful existence in Neuhaldensleben was wrapped in a dense silver web in which the commonplace timorously hid in the face of the marvelous and in which reality meant nothing, the soul's experience of the thrilling dream meant everything.

Did it merely constitute insignificant exaltations of the lonely young girl?

Yes — exaltations they were, perhaps even morbid and dangerous. But did they not also contain the drive toward artistic creation? After all, were my imaginary experiences not colorful and concrete enough for me to think of times that I had experienced them in reality? And yet I must say that they contained nothing sultry or sensually exciting. At bottom, I was still a pure, unawakened child, and so I was content

57

to share like a sister the bold and strange life of this man and to become the understanding, gentle and resigned female for whom he had been searching in vain until now. I did not have the slightest chance to see him face to face, much less to approach him in any way. For one, I did not even have the money to travel close to his inviolably secluded abode. I constantly imagined how I could do so despite all obstacles — but did I really want it? My feeling had gradually turned into love — if one can call love a feeling which absorbs all your inner strength, and an existence in a world which you carry in your own breast and which totally possesses you.

But, for my sensitive nature, the greatest magic of my love was the impossibility of it coming into conflict with the real world. I could not be disappointed because the bottomlessly deep eyes of my fairy prince would never look at me with a cold, rejecting glance; my blissful absorption could not be disturbed by a rational word. . . . But my longing to confess to her did not abate. To come closer to her by confessing my deepest feeling seemed sweetly enticing. Also, the unusual aspect of my secret must appeal to her poetic senses. So I vacillated between flight and coming closer. Disturbed and at the same time delighted, I felt how she began to occupy herself with me, and then how through our glances, our smiles, we began to commune with each other.

An evening came when the absence of her husband and my mother, who had probably gone to the theatre, left us alone undisturbed. The children were asleep. Elizabeth was a little unwell and sat in a deep armchair. Above the desk surrounded by ivy a large carved wooden crucifix looked down on us, and I felt as if I were about to make a great and terrible sacrifice of my self.

She asked and I answered. Although I fought desperately against surrendering my secret, I actually wanted to do so. Confessions always resemble a love struggle. A grappling, one against the other — until one succumbs devotedly, afraid and yet satisfied."

When Gabriele whispers that she is in love with a man she has never seen in real life, Elizabeth immediately sympathizes with the young girl and, contrary to Gabriele's mother, is not upset. She assumes Gabriele is merely experiencing the same type of crush she herself used to feel as a young girl for various young men. None of her crushes had prevented her, however, from accepting her present husband, a successful artist, when he proposed to her; she was certain Gabriele would do the same.

"I shook my head, and when she saw how I trembled, she began to understand that this might be something different, more serious than a teenage crush. Gradually, the poignancy of my tale began to affect her, as I had predicted; she showed much tender understanding with the result of tightening the bonds which tied me to her. For she enjoyed ruling over people, and in this instance she felt that a struggling soul had surrendered to her without conditions."

When she is around twenty, Gabriele falls in love with an artist she has known for some time. Her intense and very secret feelings are unrequited, and she suffers to the point of a physical breakdown. Gabriele says about herself:

"That one could approach a male outside the family context, I would not have imagined even in my wildest dreams. My imagination had not been revived by erotic literature or by any murky novels. At the bottom of my heart, I was a twenty-year-old child who was telling herself fairy tales.

However, underneath all that innocent play lived a powerful, terrible force which I myself did not comprehend. I would have been incapable of approaching a man, yet I could give my life for him and I could die with longing for him."

The young girl actually becomes seriously ill and recuperates only because of her mother's utmost dedication and care.

After recuperating from this episode, Gabriele has to take over the household and make do with very little money. Her father has died, her mother is ailing and Gabriele has to care for her four younger brothers for several years. She has little time for romantic fantasies. When three of her brothers leave home, Gabriele moves to Weimar with her mother and youngest brother in order to be closer to Elizabeth and her family. Elizabeth's husband is a well-known artist and is surrounded by stimulating people. Gabriele is happy in Weimar and leads an exciting social life, going to many parties and summer outings.

"I was disappointed when Elizabeth stayed away from such excursions, which she hated; nevertheless, I was much surer and gayer without her presence. What I loved most of all was roaming with her alone through the park in the moonlight and listening to her singing an old folksong in her gentle, dark voice. This ability to become ecstatic in the enjoyment of nature united us more deeply than anything else. I did not envy my friend Hedwig her male conquests. . . .

The fragrance of linden blossoms lay sweet and heavy over the summer evening, and a golden glimmer of the setting sun glistened peacefully above the tree tops. Slowly, people wandered along the park meadows, and each lover's hands stealthily searched for the other's. And soulmates' eyes shone with peace and quiet joy at their mutual understanding.

Like transparent winged creatures, yellow blossom leaves drifted through the air onto my outstretched hand, and I shared their gentle dying with the beloved woman by my side."

After several years, Elizabeth and her husband experience financial difficulties. At that time Elizabeth gives birth to her fifth child. Gradually, her life overwhelms her, and she suffers from what the doctors diagnose as a case of hysteria. Gradually, she deteriorates.

"I had a thousand proofs that my mother was burning with jealousy toward the woman to whom I had given the best part of my heart. My mother shared the opinion of most people that Elizabeth's illness consisted merely of a series of imaginings, that it could be cured through will power, and that she took advantage of me in order to fully make me her slave.

I knew differently — and yet I had seen a hint of relief in Elizabeth's eyes when there was talk of my leaving town. There comes a time between people who are very close, in which the scrutiny of love, the knowledge that the other one can see through you into your most secret hiding places, becomes a torture."

Gabriele, no longer young and still unmarried, and her mother decide to move to Munich, the city of bohemians and those who want to liberate themselves from the confines of bourgeois existence. Gabriele returns for a visit with Elizabeth.

"Our being together was full of a calm composure. We understood, without having to discuss it, why we had to separate. When I left in the evening, she accompanied me to the station. She was full of love, and she told me that nothing could hurt our union. And yet a fine coolness hovered between us. She was not unhappy that I was leaving. Or did she want to make it easier for me to leave? I never saw Elizabeth again."

from   THE NEW EVE:
        "Modern Education and Old Morality"

            by Maria Janitschek

                            (Leipzig, Hermann Seemann, 1906)

Maria Janitschek implicitly rejects the theories of congenital lesbianism. She seems to have been familiar with the predecessors of Freud whose works were discussed in the Yearbook of Intermediate Sexual Types, *E. Gley and Dr. Arduin, and perhaps with Freud's own 1905 essay, "The Sexual Aberrations." Like Freud, Janitschek shows that lesbianism is "caused" by a faulty environment which encourages the homosexual side of an individual's natural bisexuality to become dominant. Seffi is raised as a boy, made to have little regard for her female sexuality, taught that sex with men is dirty and dangerous and that all her heterosexual instincts must be repressed. Since she had not been explicitly taught to feel such anxiety about her homosexual instincts, they take over and she falls in love with another girl.*

"Since her eighth year, when her parents had died, Seffi had been living with the family of her father's oldest friend, Mr. Steffert. 'If we have room for seven, we'll find a little nook for an eighth person,' he thought. Frau Steffert, a *zaftig* Rubenesque type of woman, had looked worried: 'One girl amongst seven boys, and with me not having the slightest time for supervision. What is going to happen?' But her wise, good heart made her think of a way out. 'The little one's simply going to be treated exactly like the boys.' This is how she invalidated any scruples.

And every morning, come winter or summer, Seffi was made to take a cold shower; if she refused, she received a hiding; she was made to sleep summer and winter under a thin blanket with the window wide

                            61

open, and she had to share the heaviest kind of work with the servant girls and such. Nobody cared about her intellectual development. She knew how to read and write; Sundays she went to church with the rest of the family, and every Christmas she received from her foster mother six shiny gold pieces, which were put into her savings box. She was excellent at doing housework; however, not even her foster mother's slaps could make her sew or do any type of work requiring meticulous details. In these cases her brothers would come to her rescue; they were all equally fond of her. Frau Steffert's experiment in education was full of risks. Often during the summer, when they all went swimming in the nearby lake and walked into the water just as God had created them — Mama, alone, was the exception — the maturing Seffi would hesitate before she'd let her last piece of clothing fall at the shore. The mother, who was already practicing her swimming arts in the midst of her sons, would always scold her.

'Well, are you coming? Don't make such a fuss!' And then when Seffi jumped resolutely into the water, the energetic mother would move close to her.

'It actually looks as if you were ashamed! Maybe you think the boys are looking at you? You silly thing! What about you could anybody possibly want to look at?'

And Seffi secretly agreed with her mother and felt secure in her great natural innocence. Since she hated sewing, and since her clothes suffered badly from doing housework as well as from her youthful wrestling matches with her brothers, she wore as little as possible. Besides her dress, she wore only an undershirt. Not more and not less, come summer or winter. More than once a day, the thin cotton dress would fly up when she jumped down the stairs or when she chased around the courtyard, and her tanned, slender Diana thighs would become visible. Nobody found this offensive, least of all she herself. Her brothers were used to treating her exactly as one of their own. When they wrestled, they punched her just like all the others, without worrying where their fists landed.

Up until two weeks ago she had shared a bedroom with the two youngest boys. Hans had often slipped into her bed; they had pinched each other and pulled each other's hair and had thought of nothing but childish nonsense. Then, all of a sudden, when the warm spring winds began to blow and all plants began to sprout, Mama Steffert realized that Seffi's breasts were growing tremendously. She did not say anything, but when Karl moved out of his little upstairs room, she told her foster daughter very curtly that from now on she was to sleep upstairs. Seffi was only too happy to get away from the playful banter of her roommates and moved upstairs. The moment the significant separation had taken place, Seffi's person took on a mysterious aspect for the boys. Her former bedroom had been next door to that of the oldest brothers, and they had to pass through to get outside. At all hours of the night, one or the other of them had slipped through without considering Seffi, who slept soundly and who looked like a boy herself beside the other two boys. Now she was lying upstairs. Whatever for? Wasn't she going to be sad to be so far away from the brothers? Nobody was going to tease her, pull her beautifully shaped toes, or whisper all sorts of nonsense into her ears."

The brothers take turns sneaking into Seffi's room. One of them is caught in the process by the irate Mrs. Steffert. She orders him downstairs and gives Seffi two powerful slaps. The brothers nevertheless manage to sneak up secretly. One of them brings Casanova's memoirs and Boccaccio, and the two giggle and gloat over the forbidden literature. Seffi's sexual instincts are awakened by this reading and by the desire she awakens in the young men, who keep watch on each other to prevent any one of them from endangering Seffi's virginity. Mrs. Steffert, too, impresses upon Seffi the importance of retaining her virginity. She "took Seffi aside and described to her in the most vivid colors the disgrace a young girl experiences if she becomes a mother: 'You have to give birth naked in front of a group of medical students in the clinic, for I would chase you out of my home immediately.'

After such descriptions Seffi swore to herself to keep her virginity, even if her warm blood screamed for fulfillment.

During summer vacation a niece of Mrs. Steffert came for a visit. She was a delicate blonde girl who sought refuge with Seffi when the playful pranks of the boys scared her. Frau Steffert gave in to Agathe's pleas to have her bed put up in Seffi's room. For the time being, the cupboard was stored in the hallway. The lovely, small, still entirely innocent Agathe knew no more about life than any six-year-old child, although she was all of sixteen. For Seffi the arrival of this sunny companion meant a great relief. For one thing none of the boys could attack her any longer (the thought of them had secretly bothered her constantly), and then she had someone of her own sex to whom she could fully open her heart. In their white little shirts they took turns crawling into each other's beds, where they exchanged thoughts on all kinds of subjects. Agathe was amazed at the great wisdom of her friend. One evening, when Agathe had already wished her good night and was just at the point of falling asleep, Seffi suddenly started crying;

and Agathe, fully awakened by her friend's sobbing, returned once more to her bed. She stroked her and caressed her and took hold of Seffi's tightly clenched hands.

What was the matter? Agathe inquired. Things couldn't be better, could they? Everyone loved her and she, Agathe, was especially fond of her. With those words she pressed herself close to Seffi and embraced her fervently. At this moment Seffi became calm and closed her troubled eyes. A soft, tender expression stole across her face. Breast to breast, they fell asleep.

Some time later, during lunch, Alfred made a remark to Seffi, who sat beside Agathe, but Seffi was engrossed in the contemplation of a little blonde curl which hung on her friend's forehead and gently vibrated with each heartbeat.

Alfred turned to his mother and whispered something. Both of them observed the two young girls, and then Alfred laughed disdainfully.

Fearing his parents, Alfred had had to suffer silently the suspicion that his oldest brother was trying to gain Seffi's favors for himself. He could see relinquishing her to another man, but to a girlfriend — never.

He had stirred up his mother's suspicions. From now on she observed the two young girls without cessation. She discovered that Agathe became livelier, more passionate, when she was with Seffi, that both looked into each other's eyes for unnecessarily long periods, and that they caressed each other more than was customary between young girls; that each kept trying to stay close to the other and became sad when they had to be apart.

A week later Frau Steffert called Seffi into the living room and fastened her eyes on her in a most penetrating way.

'Starting today, Agathe is going to sleep in the guest room downstairs; have her things brought down, and be sure that the cupboard will be put back into your room.' Seffi's slender figure trembled. Her beautiful brown eyes filled with tears.

'Leave her with me, leave her with me!' She raised her hands imploringly to the tall woman who stood before her like a judge.

'No, you shameless thing, down she'll come. Do you think I don't see through you?' As was her habit, her hands jerked as if they were getting ready to strike a good blow. All color vanished from Seffi's tanned cheeks. 'Quick! Get out!' Frau Steffert nudged her roughly. At this moment Seffi threw her arms around her neck.

'Mother, from the time I was small, you have trained me to look at everything in nature without flinching. You beat me when I lowered my eyes. Nothing was to be spared me; you made me look at the artery and every pulsating nerve of a procreating nature, a nature which has no desire but procreation. There was to be no toning down, no veils for me. To see, to get to know all in its rawness was your slogan. Mother, I am young and strong; one day I myself felt the desire which every natural creature carries within. Responding to my burning desire for love, young arms opened up to me, but then you called out your halt! I would be a whore if I followed nature, which only the day before you praised as pure and great, and with blows and abuse you chased me from you. Mother,' she put her trembling lips close to the ear of the woman, 'it is you who has driven me into the arms of my friend. Leave her to me now.' "

from   ON CYPRESS

by Marie-Madeleine
(Baroness von Puttkamer)

(Berlin, Vita, 1895)

The poems of Marie-Madeleine (Baroness von Puttkamer) show the influence of French decadent literature, especially the poetry of Baudelaire and Verlaine and their disciple Pierre Louÿs. Lesbian love is seen in glitteringly erotic terms − but it usually brings death and destruction in its wake. At its best it involves the corruption of a young innocent. The Baroness' poems suggest to what extent some lesbian writers internalized the male view of lesbian evil by the end of the nineteenth century.

We would like to acknowledge the assistance of Frankie Hucklenbroich in rendering these poems into English.

SAPPHO

Gently, the ocean waves
sing their eternal dirge
and softly the humid spring night
enfolds me. My soul
searches for you.

Oh, come, sweet flocks of girls!
I want to drink of your beauty.
Give your wild hair to the wind,
and drop your raiments
silently.

My pale child, give me your mouth, and feed
my own mad fires. How cool
your red lips are. You haven't learned how love
feels yet.

And you, with your thick mane of red-gold curls
flowing almost to your heels,
like waves of flame,
show me the fires that glitter and flicker
from your eyes. You must not ever leave me,
for you are as beautiful
as the glowing sun.

And you two shy and slender sisters
are pale as moonlight,
with your quiet heartache
and your silent pangs of love.

With your limbs' marble splendor
shining white as the waves' glimmering foam,
and your hair the night,
you are more silent
than a dream.

Oh, bouquet of blossoms! Oh, flock of girls!
I want to drink of your beauty.
Give your wild hair to the wind,
and drop your raiments
silently.

VAGABONDS

You will leave house
and hearth
for the sake of my eyes' dark glow.
You will be despised
and dishonored,
like a beggar.
And you will throw your happiness and your fame
into the dusty street. I will be
your only possession!

At night when the streetlamps, with their flame-red stars,
peer tiredly through the fog,
we will wander through the streets, work
and sweet sin
surging noisily around us,
and lust and hunger, like the sea!

On and on we will wander,
listening reverently to the wild waltz-melodies
and to what the silken dresses rustle, and to what
the lace shirts whisper, and what the sweet, wild,
curling, long hair of girls
crackles.

Then, the fever-roses
will bloom brightly on our cheeks
and all our senses will open,
though our longing won't die!
Grinning, we will drink the cup of life
that brims with pain . . .

And hate and mockery surrounding us,
and everyone condemning us, and all the preachers
threatening us with punishment
and hell-fire, we are
forever damned! And yet, you will leave
house and hearth
for my eyes' weariness . . .

WORDS OF OLD AGE

I cannot sleep at night. I cannot.
When my tired eyes
have barely closed, youth
appears to me in dreams.

A naked, regal, blonde woman,
wild lust bright in her glances:
So like springtime her body blossoms,
her white breasts, so like god!

She stares at me with a mad laugh,
a bawdy, echoing peal.
I hear her laughter everywhere; so sweet
and so full of scorn.

Oh, how wildly she mocks me!
Her body blossoms so like springtime,
a young, young, young woman . . .
I cannot sleep at night.

CRUCIFIXA

I saw you tortured on a stake,
high on a dark cross I saw you tied.
The marks of my sinful kisses
glowed on your white flesh like purple wounds.

How slender your young limbs are,
and how childish your budlike breasts!
But in your eyes, my blonde child,
burn the torches of wild lust.

And yet, you were cool, white velvet,
stainless as a sharpened sword,
when your young innocence enflamed me
and I desired you so boundlessly.

I gave you of my own poison,
and I gave you my poison's strength.
And now that you are fully ablaze
my soul shudders at what I have done.

I want to kneel before the altars
my own wanton daring destroyed . . .
Madonna with a whore's eyes
I myself crucified you!

FELICITA VON VESTVALI

by Rosa von Braunschweig

(From *Yearbook of Intermediate Sexual Types,*
Volume I, 1903)

Rosa von Braunschweig accepts the views of the sexologists of the late nineteenth century: homosexuality is congenital, and this abnormality usually manifests itself in childhood, the lesbian girl always showing distinctly masculine tastes. But Braunschweig argues too that such masculine traits might permit a woman to realize the genius that is within her. And she presents her idol, Felicita von Vestvali, as a role model of courage and intelligence for other "Uranian" women.

The source material which gives us reliable information about the lives of women with Uranian tendencies is by far scarcer than that about their male colleagues, not because this peculiar tendency is less frequent amongst women – it occurs far more frequently than one might guess – but because women exercise more restraint. This is a result of their education, for even as children, girls are trained toward greater modesty than are boys, and this sensitivity prevents them later, when their sexual drives become active, from disclosing themselves.

It is true, in Germany homosexual love between women is not threatened by any legal paragraph, but socially women suffer perhaps even more from prejudice than men, since the ignorant masses brand their inclination usually as base sensuality. How different it would be if parents became enlightened about the nature of homosexuality and learned to recognize that it is imparted by nature. They could then easily recognize the peculiar tendency even in the child – for example, when girls are more interested in boys' games than in their dolls, and when in their later development distinct traces of a masculine nature show up. If finally some unimportant circumstances causes the homosexual tendency to surface clearly, parents could guide their daughters' seemingly irrational behavior into a positive direction. How often girls are driven into a marriage in which not only they but also a second person becomes unhappy. If parents would learn to recognize their children's sexual tendency from behavior which is contrary to their own sex, and if they could then mildly and justly judge this tendency, much misery could be prevented in the world.

That a Uranian tendency does not necessarily ruin or debilitate one's character is borne out by innumerable examples. After all, the female Uranian usually combines specifically feminine traits, such as sensitivity and depth of feeling, with masculine energy, drive, and goal-oriented striving; at the same time she is free of pettiness, vanity, and the dependency of women; on the other hand, she quite frequently is outfitted with the actual sensuality and carelessness of man — however, heterosexuals are not perfect people either. In any case, the combination of masculine and feminine qualities — formed under favorable conditions — quite often makes for beings whose talents far surpass those of mother-women, and who contribute to the arts and sciences just as valuable services as do women who are dedicated to the propagation of the species.

One of those extraordinary beings was Felicita von Vestvali. She filled the Old and the New World with her fame, and it was mostly due to her Uranian nature that she knew how to overcome all obstacles with masculine energy and that her boundless striving allowed her to achieve the goal to which her genius had predestined her.

It frequently has been maintained that she was a female hermaphrodite. She encountered countless hostilities from the lords of creation, who used every insinuation possible to put her down. For rebuttal we want to declare with certainty that all rumors which have been invented regarding her hermaphroditism belong in the realm of fairy tales. She was even the mother of a daughter who still lives in America.

It happens frequently that totally homosexual women do not recognize their nature until they have been initiated into the mysteries of love by a man. This is what happened to Felicita von Vestvali. However, after she had been enlightened more thoroughly, she, like many other Uranian women, considered the continuation of an intimate intercourse with man to be immoral, since it quite definitely contradicted her innermost feelings. Naturally, she painfully felt the conflict with all existing moral laws, but truth toward her self was for

74

her more important than a moral code which was made without consideration for the third sex, whose existence simply cannot be denied and about whom famous scientists are now trying to inform the public.

Felicita von Vestvali's real name was Anna Marie Staegemann. She was the youngest daughter of a higher government official in Stettin, and she was born there on February 25, 1829. The peculiarity of her nature showed itself from the beginning. As a child, for example, she wanted to become a missionary priest. When the schoolroom in her parents' home was empty, she crept in, stood on the podium, and proceeded to preach with an enthusiasm far beyond her age how she was going to better mankind. Once her father listened to her from the yard and then embraced his child with tears in his eyes. At different times she chased around with her brothers like the wildest boy.

Fearlessness and generosity were her fundamental character traits until her death, and they were manifested during her childhood. Quite often, when her strict father intended to punish one of her brothers or sisters, she stepped forward and took punishment upon herself. When she discovered the theatre, she became consumed with the glowing desire to become an actress, but as happens so frequently, her parents wanted to hear nothing of it. Without much ado, she ran away in boys' clothes. She found employment with the Broekelmann Traveling Company. The director, an old hand with the theatre, soon recognized the young girl's extraordinary talent and wanted to keep her tied to his company. However, Felicita, or Maria, as she was then called, soon felt a pull away from the provincial conditions. She found an engagement in Leipzig, and there became a protégé of the famous Wilhelmine Schroeder-Devrient. Under her direction she sang rather successfully parts like Agathe, the Daughter of the Regiment, and finally even Norma. However, her spirit which strove toward highest perfection, felt the lack of real skill; the audience was merely delighted by her youthful voice. In order to engage in thorough voice training, she went to the Paris Conservatory. She studied with untiring devotion, but at the same time she fully enjoyed life. And here it was that a friend enlightened her about her Uranian inclination. As much as her lively nature craved the joy of love, she nevertheless considered love merely a flower which decorated her life's path; the essence of her striving, however, was dedicated to her profession. Therefore she accepted the offer of a larger concert tour before the completion of her studies. The tour, which took her to the Isle of Jersey, was abruptly interrupted because the impresario made off with the cash box. With quick determination, our young artist took up residence as a singing instructor and played the organ in church every Sunday. Her enterprising spirit, combined with her youthfully beautiful appearance, helped her become a brilliant success. However, after one winter she continued studying voice with Mercadante in Naples. Under his guidance her voice developed into a contralto of such phenomenal depth that speculating impresarios advised her to study tenor parts; however, doctors declared that her voice would be able to stand this experiment for ten years at the most. That was not enough for her ambition. In order to train her heavy voice also for lighter music, she went to study with the famous voice teacher Romani, who then lived in Florence, and appeared for the first time publicly at the Scala in Milan, singing the part of Azucena in the premiere of Verdi's *Trovatore.* She now assumed the name Felicita von Vestvali. Her next parts were Romeo in Bellini's *Romeo and Juliet* and *Tancred.* Her success was grandiose. Then she sang in various concerts in London and was fêted by the English aristocracy as few singers before her. She became a close friend of Lord and Lady Palmerston.

The land of her dreams, however, was America, and in 1854 she set sail for there. Immediately after her first performance she became a veritable cult figure with the Yankees. She was compared to the American goddess of liberty, and she was called Vestvali the Magnificent. In New York she received a monthly salary of ten thousand francs. Then followed a tour through all the major American cities.

In Mexico City the famous singer and director of the National Theatre, Henriette Sonntag, had died, and Vestvali was offered the theatre with an annual subsidy of forty-five thousand dollars. She returned to Europe to establish a select company. When they arrived in Mexico City, the entire city was decorated as for a national holiday; President Caminfort received her together with his top government officials; she was presented with six magnificent horses, a great celebration at the palace Iturbid, and a torchlight parade. Truly these are honors which have seldom been shown to a woman, an artist.

Counting on her great popularity, she attempted in Mexico City to sing in Spanish the part of Figaro in Rossini's *Barber of Seville.* When the revolution erupted, she could not be paid the whole subsidy, and she was given a piece of land which even now carries her name.

Tired of the exhausting life she had been leading, she returned to Italy to recuperate. However, she had but a short rest period. The new theatre in Piacenza was to be dedicated, and she was asked to participate in the first performance. Then she was offered an engagement at the Paris opera, where she competed with and surpassed several excellent singers, such as the famous Tietjans. Emperor Napoleon even presented her with a solid silver armor for her performance as Romeo.

She remained in Paris for two years, and her salon became the meeting ground for all who claimed to have a name in the literary world, as well as for the aristocracy. Many beautiful women competed for Vestvali's favor, and many a husband had reason to be jealous of the beautiful, chivalrous Romeo.

However, America beckoned to her again. There she wanted to give a performance of Gluck's *Orpheus*. Felicita should have known the taste of Americans: the tasteful, classic music of the old master Gluck did not appeal to the Yankees. The undertaking proved a failure. Time, trouble, and money had been wasted, and Vestvali withdrew full of bitterness to a villa in the magnificent surroundings of San Francisco.

In order to recuperate, she studied the part of Hamlet, about which she had been enthusiastic for years. She had been taking both this play and the *Romeo* of the great British playwright on all of her trips, for even while singing opera, she had embued Bellini's *Romeo* with a Shakespearean spirit.

At that time the first male lover of the San Francisco theater fell ill, and Vestvali was being besieged to appear as Romeo. The bad success of *Orpheus* had taken away her taste for opera, and she now enthusiastically seized the opportunity to go into the theatre and to embody this ideal youth in dramatic form and in the English language. The audience received her enthusiastically, and once again she triumphantly visited the cities of America. Besides the part of Romeo, she had added several male and female parts to her repertoire.

From this time she dates her friendship with a Miss E. L., a German actress to whom she left the larger part of her fortune. Although this relationship lasted until her death, it did not bring her sheer happiness.

In 1868 Vestvali gave a guest performance at the Royal Lyceum Theatre in London. She performed Hamlet twenty times and Romeo twenty-two times, as well as Petruchio in *The Taming of the Shrew*. Here again, she received outstanding honors. Queen Victoria received Vestvali in a private audience. Lord Bulver claimed never to have seen a more ingenious rendition of Hamlet, and the English newspapers called her the "female Kean." The Union of Art in London nominated Vestvali as an honorary member, a distinction she had long ago received from "Santa Cecile" in Rome.

Up until then the German artist had achieved all her successes only in foreign languages. She had sung in Italian, French, and Spanish, and she had performed on the dramatic stage in English. Suddenly, the German spirit awakened in her. After having filled both hemispheres with her fame, she wanted to show her fatherland what a genius could achieve with untameable creative drive and extraordinary energy.

Frequently, she had been advised to the contrary. Unfortunately, Germany is the country which least gives license to the extraordinary, even if it is justified because of intellectual and physical superiority. But Vestvali would not let herself be deterred. In Hamburg she first performed the part of Hamlet in German. The larger public immediately received her enthusiastically, but the press had much to criticize, amongst other things that her pronunciation contained a trace of an American accent. She worked diligently until the mother tongue she had not used for so long once again became easy to pronounce. When she played Hamlet, the flaw had been eliminated.

The well-known Leipzig critic Gottschell wrote:

The female Hamlet. Guest performance by Felicita von Vestvali. It seems certain that the larger part of the audience who yesterday attended the debut came merely for strangeness' sake and in part even to destroy a lady who was brave enough to play Hamlet. When Vestvali first appeared as Hamlet, she was received silently. The noble figure, who surpassed the king and many of the other 'heroes' in height and all of them in nobility of posture, her expressive face turned toward the floor, already disarmed all prejudice. The second doubt was dissipated when she began to speak. Her sonorous alto voice, her clear declamation which showed no trace of dialect, indicated that the artist was equal to her task also in this respect, and the first act was by far not yet over before she received enthusiastic applause which soon increased to such a degree that the guest performer received some eighteen final curtain calls. The power of her genius caused all scruples against women acting male parts to be forgotten; the impression which this Hamlet made was powerful. Miss von Vestvali showed him to be not only a dreamer, but she also vividly represented his energetic will, his pressing, piercing decision toward action, and his vacillating until the moment of the execution. The most important scene was probably the struggle at Ophelia's grave and the eruption of his love for her. And, not to forget the technical aspect at the expense of artistic interpretation: we have never witnessed better fencing on stage.

Miss Vestvali continued her successful guest performances in Leipzig as Romeo, as Elizabeth in Laube's *Essex*, and as Isabella in *The Bride of Messina*. Laube himself pronounced her to be one of the best performers of the past

From Leipzig, Vestvali gave a guest performance at the National Theatre in Berlin — the same theatre which burned to the ground years ago and is remembered only by the older theatre audience — and gained the favor of the metropolis, thereby finally achieving full artistic recognition for all of Germany.

A much feared critic of the *Berline Daily Blade*, wrote:

National Theatre. On January 20: *Hamlet, Prince of Denmark*. Hamlet, Miss von Vestvali as guest performer.

A blond youth from Nordic lands, with light colored hair and fresh, healthy coloring, although from birth a little hypochondriacal — this is Felicita von Vestvali's Hamlet. He is rightfully one of the most famous and doubtlessly most original and ingenious achievements in the realm of the theatre — indeed he stands alone in kind and significance.

For the outward representation of a female Hamlet Mother Nature probably had not gifted any other woman, none, with such splendid genius and specifically "masculine" traits. Her physique alone reminds one of the — so called — Lord of Creation. With it comes a powerful vocal organ which often seems deeper than a tenor.

Concerning the artistic interpretation of the part, we already suggested an opinion: amongst the approximately two dozen Hamlets we have seen in the course of the years, the one of our guest performer's was definitely the most original. Again, we are not speaking about the external appearance but merely about the intellectual aspect; we are not speaking about the husk but the kernel of the achievement.

We also have before us the pronouncement of one of the most popular Austrian poets:

An extraordinary talent, such as Vestvali, is justified in giving full reign to her vulcanic genius. Neither custom nor restrictive aesthetic rules can be of any importance for the expressive need of such a boundlessly artistic nature. The fact that this is so constitutes by no means an artistic sacrilege. There is no sense in lamenting her unorthodox acting, as some critics do. Vestvali's remarkable intelligence puts all attacks to shame.

We have quoted the press from the most important cities which indicates how victoriously Vestvali emerged from the many hostilities she encountered. For many years she traveled through Germany and continuously performed with the greatest success.

But the great strain she experienced throughout her life had a negative influence on her health. More and more often she was forced to rest. She withdrew to her villa in Warmbrunn. However, a life without any action was impossible for her; when art did not claim her, she threw herself into speculating on building construction. In Warmbrunn she built the entire Russian colony. When she visited her married sister in Warsaw, she bought land there and ordered and supervised construction. Her health could not withstand all this strain. An incurable disease weakened her and made an early end to this rich, eventful life. She died in Warmbrunn on April 3, 1880, in her fifty-second year of life.

We shall quote a few excerpts from letters to a young actress with whom she shared a true friendship until her death. Faithful friendship was a fundamental trait of her noble and idealistic nature, and those whom she honored with her friendship remained attached to this extraordinary person with touching reverence. She often called herself "Hamlet," just as she addressed that young actress — I am that actress — as "Horatio" when she wrote to her. The letters give short glimpses of her artistic views as well as of her Uranian nature. In one of the letters she writes:

Oh, it is terribly boring to give guest performances from city to city. I'm beginning to feel like the village custodian who walks around with the collection bag. Amen! — if only one continues to reap rich contributions, says E. [her longtime friend and companion*] then it's all right. That's a fine attitude for an idealistic bel esprit, isn't it, Horatio? Yes, I would like to have a regular theatre in Berlin and nowhere else except perhaps America. Oh, if it weren't for the damned long trip, I would have been over there ages ago. Adventure simply appeals to me — I am the way I am.

The last letter which she wrote to me from her sickbed in Warsaw is as follows:

How everything has changed from the way I expected it to be! My

---

*author's note

nervous disease, which is terrible, has been softened by G's presence. [G. was Vestvali's last love; however Vestvali could not separate from her friend E. because of financial complications, and Vestvali was too honorable to press for a dissolution.*] She is divinely good. You can trust me, Horatio, I don't feel my sufferings half as much when she is with me. I love her passionately and I want to do something nice for her day in and day out. Now it doesn't matter whether it happened under the peach or the apple tree, whether she seduced me or I her — we love each other passionately. I just wish you were here, dear Horatio. You would be delighted with us. Do you remember our evening's conversation a propos G. at Charlotten Street? G. will soon write to you personally. She has to go to the train station to pick up E. and she has not slept all night. She sleeps in a bed adjacent to mine. Both of us greet you warmly and I press you to my heart in old friendship.

Yours,
Hamel-fett (Muttonfat)

Vestvali, who became ill while visiting her sister in Warsaw, was nursed by a Miss G. with touching care, and only toward the end Miss E. came to nurse her also. While Vestvali's relationship with E. was no longer a happy one, she nevertheless was unable to dissolve it, despite the fact that her whole heart belonged to G. This discord depressed Vestvali very much, although she managed to treat the whole matter with a certain sense of humor, as proven by the above letter. The love Miss G. had for Vestvali is shown in the following letter:

Dear Horatio. Feli is getting worse and worse. Yesterday evening she had such raging pains in her back and her right arm that she groaned loudly; then she moaned softly and asked God for help so that one's heart wanted to break. The doctors now say that she is suffering from the old illness and also from extreme anemia. And not to be able to help, to see one's beloved end such a horrible way! She wants to let E. come and I cannot advise her against it since everything excites her so terribly. Perhaps we'll soon meet in Berlin, dear Horatio. Don't be frightened if I turn up at your house early in the morning.

A thousand greetings from your G.

Let us now finish the picture which I have painted of Vestvali in

---

*author's note

these pages. She was a person of outstanding intellect, feeling, and talent, and nobody who ever came in closer contact with her was ever able to forget the magic of her personality. The captivating amiability of her nature was a result of her great naturalness, for despite her great success she was free of all arrogance. She was happy to help those with talent who strove, but she hated dilettantes. She never emphasized her Uranian inclination; and this is why even those men who disliked this inclination felt drawn to her talent, and many a comradely tie existed between her and some excellent representatives of the male sex. Women she affected in a downright fascinating manner, and it would lead beyond the framework of this little sketch to note how many times she was worshipped. In any case, Felicita von Vestvali belonged to those exceptional beings in art as well as in life whose peculiarity can be understood only by those who understand homosexuality.

WHAT INTEREST DOES THE WOMEN'S MOVEMENT HAVE IN THE HOMOSEXUAL QUESTION?

by Anna Rueling

(Speech given at the annual conference of the
Scientific Humanitarian Committee,
October 8, 1904, Prinz Albrecht Hotel, Berlin)

Rueling shows the influence Krafft-Ebing and his disciples had on her era regarding the "third sex," the unhealthy offspring of the homosexual who is foolish enough to have children, and the masculinity of the Uranian woman — which explains her physical yearning toward other women. While attempting to enlist the sympathy and support of the women's movement, Rueling's emphasis is on how different lesbians are from heterosexual women — an approach which is diametrically opposite that of lesbian-feminists of our era. Rueling does not fail, however, to point out that lesbians have given great service to the women's movement and have earned the right to be served by the movement.

The women's movement is necessary to the history of civilization. Homosexuality is a necessity in terms of natural history, representing the bridge, the natural and obvious link between men and women. This, now, is a scientific fact against which ignorance and intolerance struggle in vain. Nevertheless, some will ask why I mention the history of civilization and natural history in one breath, two fields which upon cursory examination seem to be diametrically opposed. There is a basis for this broader view.

In general, when homosexuality is discussed, one thinks only of the Uranian men and overlooks the many homosexual women who exist and about whom much less is said because — I would almost like to say "unfortunately" — they don't have to fight an unjust penal code which resulted from false moral views. Women are not threatened with painful trials and imprisonment when they follow their inborn drive for love. But the mental stress that Uranian women endure is just as great, or greater, than the burden under which Uranian men suffer. To the world which bases its judgment on outward appearances, these women are much more obvious than even the most effeminate man. Only too often, misdirected morality exposes them to scorn and mockery.

Uranian women, even if they are not discussed, are important for our entire social structure because they influence it in many ways. Upon consideration of the facts, one must conclude that homosexuality and the women's movement are not opposed to each other, but rather that they are destined to help each other find justice and recognition and to abolish the injustice against which they now struggle.

The homosexual movement fights for the rights of all homosexuals, men as well as women. The Scientific-Humanitarian Committee is distinguished from the other movement groups which have or should have an interest in this struggle, in that it has dedicated itself enthusiastically to the Uranian woman as well as the Uranian man.

The women's movement strives for long-neglected women's rights; it is fighting especially for the greatest possible independence for women and their legal equality with men both in and out of marriage. The latter is of particular importance, first of all because of present economic conditions, and second, because the statistically proven surplus of women in the population of our country means that a large number of women simply cannot get married. Since only 10 percent of these women inherit sufficient means to live, the other 90 percent are forced to enter the labor market to earn their living in some sort of occupation. The position and participation of homosexual women in the women's movement and the movement's attempts to solve these problems are significant and deserve extensive, universal attention.

One must distinguish between two facets of the homosexual woman, her general personality and her sexual proclivity. Her overall personality is of primary importance; of secondary importance is the direction of her sex drive, which must be considered in all its complexity before it can be completely understood, since the physical love drive is generally an overflow, a natural result of psychological qualities, i.e., in people with primarily masculine characteristics, it naturally directs itself toward women and vice versa, regardless of the actual physical sex of the person. The homosexual woman possesses many qualities, inclinations, and capacities which we ordinarily consider masculine. She particularly deviates from the feminine norm in her emotional life. While emotion is almost always — exceptions prove the rule — the predominant and deciding trait in the heterosexual woman, clear reason rules the Uranian woman. She is, like the average man, more objective, energetic, and goal oriented than the feminine woman; her thoughts and feelings are those of a man; she does not imitate man, she is inherently similar to him, and this is the important point that the foes of the so-called "man-woman" always ignore because they never really bother to study the homosexual phenomenon. It is very easy to condemn something one does not understand, just as easy as it is difficult to correct a preconceived and wrong opinion or to allow a false notion to be changed by enlightenment.

I want to mention here that there exist both an absolute and a merely psychological homosexuality. Masculine characteristics do not necessarily result in a sexual drive toward the female sex, for each homosexual woman possesses more or less feminine characteristics, which, with the immensely diverse gradations in the transition between the sexes, can at times be expressed in a sexual drive toward a man. Of course, in these cases the drive usually exerts itself toward a very feminine man, as the natural complement to the woman with a strongly masculine soul. To support my statement, let me cite the cases of George Sand and Daniel Stern, both of whom loved men who were of the most feminine type, Frederick Chopin and Franz Liszt. Clara Schumann, the great artist, was also married to a man with strongly feminine inclinations, Robert Schumann. It appears, by the way, as though in the women I described as psychologically homosexual, the sexual drive was never very strongly developed; George Sand and Daniel Stern loved their artists far more with their souls than with their senses. To a certain extent I am therefore inclined to refer to "unsexual" natures when I speak of psychologically homosexual women.

Since the homosexual woman with her masculine proclivities will never suitably complement a masculine man, it is clear that the Uranian woman is not suited for marriage. Uranian women usually are aware of this fact, at least subconsciously, and accordingly refuse to go to the altar. But often they must deal with parents, cousins, aunts, and all the other dear friends and relatives, who tell them day in and day out about the necessity of marriage, and with this wise advice make life hell for them. Thanks to the poor education we provide for young girls, Uranian women often stumble blindly into marriage, without clear views and concepts of sexuality and sex life. As long as so-called "society" views spinsterhood as something unpleasant, even inferior, Uranian women will all too often allow outer circumstances to drive them into marriages in which they will neither give nor receive happiness. Aren't such marriages far more immoral than the love pact of two people who are drawn to each other by a powerful force?

The women's movement wants to reform marriage. It wants to bring about legal changes so that present conditions will cease to exist, so that discord and injustice, arbitrariness and slavish subjection, will disappear from the family, so that future generations will be healthier and stronger.

In connection with these attempts to reform, the women's movement must not forget the degree to which absurd attitudes toward homosexual women are responsible for tragic marriages. I specifically say "the degree to which" because naturally I do not attribute total blame to those absurd attitudes. But because even part of the blame lies there, the women's movement cannot dismiss its responsibility for informing society by spoken and written work how pernicious it is to force homosexual women into marriage. First of all, it is bad for the two people involved. The man is simply deceived because, apart from its ideal meaning, marriage is a mutual contract in which both parties assume rights and duties. However, a homosexual woman can fulfill her duties toward the man only with aversion or, at best, with indifference. A forced sexual union is doubtless a torture for both parties, and no decent, thoughtful man can see anything desirable in it, or find the happiness for which he was looking in a marriage with a Uranian woman. It often happens that the decent man then avoids sexual intercourse at home for the sake of the woman and looks for satisfaction of his sex drive in the arms of his mistress or with prostitutes. Because feminists care about the moral fiber and health of our people, they must wholeheartedly combat the pressures used to force homosexuals to marry. The women's movement can spread enlightenment which will enable society to see that the marriage of homosexuals is a triple crime; it is a crime against the state, against society itself, and against an unborn generation, for experience teaches us that the offspring of Uranians are seldom healthy and strong. The unhappy creatures who are conceived and born without love, or even desire, represent a large percentage of the mentally disturbed, retarded, epileptics, tuberculars, and degenerates of all kinds. Morbid sexual drives such as sadism and masochism are often the legacy from Uranians who procreated against their nature. The state and society should have an urgent interest in preventing Uranians from marrying, since it is the state and society who bear the burden of the care of these sick and weak beings who are unable to make any contribution in return.

It seems to me that an essentially practical point for heterosexual women to remember is that if homosexuals would remain single without damage to their social status, there would be more husbands available for those women whose natural inclinations are satisfied by the role of wife, housekeeper, and mother. Unfortunately, we still lack valid statistics regarding the number of homosexual women, but according to my intense work in this area, I believe that the statistics which resulted from Dr. Hirschfeld's studies of male homosexuality can be applied also to women. Therefore, there are approximately as many Uranian women as single women in Germany. To be more precise: say there are two million unmarried women and two million homosexual women; among these probably around 50 percent (one million) of the single women are Uranians, and around 50 percent (one million) of female homosexuals are married. They married because of social pressure, and thus blocked marriage for one million single heterosexual women. The conclusion is obvious. If more Uranian women remained single, more heterosexual women would have the opportunity to marry, which of course does not mean that this is a universal remedy against spinsterhood because there are many social conditions which are causing men to have increasing animosity toward marriage — a subject that is not relevant to our discussion here.

If the women's movement would focus on homosexuality as it relates to the marriage question, the original conception of marriage as a union between a man and woman who love each other might again come into its own. Today's too frequent marriages for money or "sensible" matches are in direct contrast to the ethical demand that people marry only for love.

I have observed that many homosexual women marry because they recognize their natural inclinations too late, and as a result they create unhappiness for themselves and others. Here too the women's movement can help, since it is very concerned with the education of the young; it can point out the importance of explaining the nature of homosexuality rationally and sensibly to older children and young people in whom homosexual tendencies have been detected by loving parents and honest, understanding friends. In this way, immense tortures and misery caused by attempts to force homosexual children into heterosexual paths could be prevented. There is no danger that effeminate heterosexual children might be considered homosexual and therefore made into homosexuals because such education would only be given after a consultation with a physician who is knowledgeable in this area. Also, experience proves that neither seduction nor anything else can transform a heterosexual into a homosexual or vice versa. Of course, a heterosexual individual can be seduced into homosexual acts, but this is a result of curiosity, craving for personal pleasure, or the need to obtain a substitute for unavailable normal intercourse. For example, the latter instance is prevalent amongst sailors, whose natural sexual drives do not change and will prevail under normal conditions.

Now, I personally want to reiterate a point frequently made by Dr. Hirschfeld, and that is that homosexuals do not belong exclusively to any particular social class; that is, homosexuality does not occur more frequently in the upper class than the lower class, or vice versa. No father or mother − not even those among you − can safely assume that there is no Uranian child among his or her offspring. There is a strange belief prevalent in the middle class that homosexuality does not exist in their circles, and from this group comes the greatest opposition to Uranian liberation. I myself remember that once in my parents' home when homosexuality became a topic of conversation, my father declared with conviction: "This sort of thing can't happen in my family!" The facts prove the opposite! Nothing else need be said!

To return to the marriage question, I would like to note that a homosexual woman almost never becomes what can be described as a "spinster." And this remarkable fact makes Uranian women more easily recognized, especially in their later years. If one looks at an unmarried homosexual woman between the age of thirty and fifty, none of the ridiculed characteristics attributed to the average single heterosexual woman can be found. This is interesting because it proves that sensible and moderate satisfaction of the sex drive also keeps women full of life, fresh and active, while absolute sexual abstinence easily causes those unpleasant qualities we find in the spinster, such as meanness, hysteria, irritability, etc.

In order to obtain for homosexuals and all women generally the opportunity to live according to their natures, it is necessary to actively aid the women's movement's efforts to expand educational opportunities and new professions for women. But what about the ancient argument of sexual superiority? I believe that with a little good will the dispute can be settled after examination of nature's intent in creating man and woman and the transitions between the two. One must conclude that it is wrong to value one sex more highly than the other − to speak of a first-class sex, man, a second-class sex, woman, and a third-class sex, the Uranian. The sexes are not of different value, they are merely of different kind. Because of this, it is clear that men, women, and Uranians are not equally suited for all professions. This is a fact the women's movement cannot change, nor does it want to.

The feminine woman has been designed by nature to become first of all wife and mother. And she has a right to be proud of this natural destiny because there is no more honorable occupation than that of mother. Naturally, the woman who is wife, or mother, or both, does not need to forget the rest of the world because of this occupation. Rather, she should participate in all aspects of public life according to her capabilities. This is one of the most attractive goals of the women's movement.

Nature has assigned different functions to the normal man (that is, the completely virile man) than to the woman. It is undeniable that the man is physically more suited for a rugged life's struggle than a woman, so that occupations are open to him that are automatically closed to a woman, for example that of the soldier and all those jobs requiring hard physical labor.

Of course, outside of such extremes there are many professions that can be practiced equally well by men or by women, depending on their individual capabilities. One of the weakest points in the logic of the opponents of the women's movement is found in their penchant for lumping all women together under the rubric "woman," failing to note that there are no two completely identical beings, and further that professional attitudes depend upon the combined masculine and feminine qualities a person possesses. Therefore we can differentiate between a feminine personality in which feminine characteristics dominate; a masculine one, in which the masculine characteristics dominate; and finally, a feminine-masculine or a masculine-feminine personality with equally masculine and feminine qualities. When nature created the different sexes, she certainly did not intend for there to be one sphere for woman − the home − and another for man − the world. Rather, the intention was for each person to fill the role appropriate to his or her own traits and abilities.

The combinations of masculine and feminine characteristics vary so much from one person to another that all children, whether masculine or feminine, should be educated for independence in the name of simple justice. This will enable the adults to decide for themselves whether their nature suits them for the home or the world, marriage or no marriage. There must be free choice available to enable women to make their own decisions to pursue an artistic or learned profession, or to feel that they are not strong enough to do so. It is the sacred responsibility of parents to avoid stereotyped upbringing for their children and to see that each is educated according to his or her individual characteristics. Of course the schools now follow established patterns, but in the future they must provide equal education for both boys and girls and discard the notion that girls have less intellectual capacity than boys.

One need not fear that equal education for boys and girls will cause increasing competition in the professions — particularly in academia, as our opponents claim. It is true that homosexual women are specially suited for the sciences because they have those qualities lacking in feminine women: greater objectivity, energy, and perseverance. Naturally, this observation does not preclude the fact that there are extremely capable heterosexual women who are doctors, lawyers, etc. Nevertheless, I must maintain that under favorable conditions most heterosexual women choose marriage. They seek a broader, more comprehensive education in order to be esteemed companions for their husbands, not just sensual love-objects, and to be wives who are respected by their husbands as intellectual equals, and accordingly granted equal rights and responsibilities in the marriage.

Therefore, men, women, and homosexuals all benefit from a more equitable upbringing and education. Men will gain rational, sensitive companions for their lives; women will gradually gain a more worthy and legally protected position; and the Uranians will be free to dedicate themselves to their chosen professions.

Just as homosexual men often prefer professions that have a feminine quality, such as women's fashions, nursing, cooking, or being servants, homosexual women also lean toward certain professions. Thus there are many homosexual women in the medical, judicial, and agricultural professions, as well as in the creative arts.

There are those who, like Weininger, maintain that all well-known, significant, or famous women in history, literature, science, or other fields were homosexual. With my earlier statements in mind, it should be unnecessary for me to emphasize my belief that this concept cannot be substantiated, for not only history but our own observations daily prove its fallacy. On the other hand, one cannot and should not deny that many noted women were indeed homosexually inclined — I'll mention only Sappho, Christine of Sweden, Sonja Kowalewska, Rosa Bonheur. However, it would be inaccurate to include Elizabeth of England and Katharine the Great of Russia among the Uranians; while the latter was probably bisexual — her many male and female "friendships" definitely point in that direction — she was definitely not purely homosexual.

Contrary to the belief of the anti-feminists that women are inferior and that only those with strong masculine characteristics are to be valued, I believe that women in general are equal to men. I am convinced, however, that the homosexual woman is particularly capable of playing a leading role in the international women's rights movement for equality. And indeed, from the beginning of the women's movement until the present day, a significant number of homosexual women assumed the leadership in the numerous struggles and, through their energy, awakened the naturally indifferent and submissive average women to an awareness of their human dignity and rights. I am unable and unwilling to name names because as long as many consider homosexuality criminal and unnatural, at best sick, ladies I could call homosexual might feel insulted. Above all, decency and duty forbid indiscretion, and neither the noble love of a Uranian suffragette nor the feelings of a heterosexual need be aired in a public forum. But anyone with the slightest bit of familiarity with homosexual traits who has been following the women's movement at all or who knows any of its leading women personally or by pictures, will find the Uranians among the suffragettes and recognize that Uranians are often noble and fine.

Considering the contributions made to the women's movement by homosexual women for decades, it is amazing that the large and influential organizations of the movement have never lifted a finger to improve the civil rights and social standing of their numerous Uranian members. It is amazing that they have done nothing, absolutely nothing, to protect many of their best-known and most deserving leaders from ridicule and scorn by enlightening the general public about the true nature of Uranianism. They could, for example, point out that homosexual proclivities express themselves often unconsciously and unintentionally in appearance, speech, deportment, movement, dress, etc., exposing the Uranian unjustly to the heartless mockery of coarse, ignorant people. Of course not all homosexual women show masculine exteriors that harmonize with their inner selves. There are many Uranian women with completely feminine appearance which they accentuate with very feminine behavior in order to escape being detected as homosexuals. This is a comedy which is bitter and painful to those who must participate.

I understand the reason for the reluctance of the women's movement to deal with this problem, although it deals very frankly with other purely sexual matters. It stems from its fear that the movement could suffer in the eyes of the still blind and ignorant masses if it took up the homosexual question by energetically supporting the human rights of Uranians. I'll frankly admit that this fear was justified during the early days of the women's movement when it had to carefully avoid losing converts, and this fear was a credible excuse for temporarily ignoring the homosexual question. Today, however, when the movement is advancing unimpeded, when no bureaucratic wisdom, no philistinism, can block its triumphant march, this failure to deal with an important question is an injustice, an injustice which the women's movement inflicts on itself. Of course, the so-called "moderate" faction of the movement will not rouse itself to support the homosexuals simply because action along this line does not appeal to them. Someday victory will be won under the banner of radicalism. It is the radicals we expect to break the spell and openly and honestly confess: Yes, there are many Uranians among us, and we are indebted to them for their energy and work, which have brought us many great successes. Not that I want all questions of the women's movement dealt with from the homosexual standpoint; it is not my wish to credit the Uranians with all or even the largest share of accomplishments — that would be just as silly as it is wrong to ignore them.

Without a doubt, the women's movement has greater and more important assignments to complete than homosexual liberation, but it can only handle the more important tasks if it does not neglect the less significant ones. Therefore, the women's movement should not place special emphasis on the homosexual question; it is not necessary to preach about the injustices done to the Uranians from every rooftop — this would only harm the movement — I understand this aspect well; it need only speak objectively about the homosexual question when addressing the sexual, official, economic, and purely human relationships of the sexes to each other. That it can do, and in so doing, it can slowly and quietly bring about enlightenment.

I am now getting to a topic with which the women's movement has been specially concerned in recent years — prostitution. From an ethical standpoint, one can think of it as one wishes; in any case, it will have to be dealt with for a long time to come. Personally, I regard prostitution as an unfortunate but necessary evil which will be impossible to eradicate as long as there are human passions, but which, if we are fortunate, we can lessen — a goal worth striving for.

An important fact that has been completely ignored by the women's movement's struggle against the increase of prostitution and its destructive companion, venereal disease, is that 20 percent of all prostitutes are homosexual. At first this may seem odd because of the contradiction between homosexuality and constant sexual intercourse with the male. This situation has been explained to me more than once by a "girl of the streets" who told me that she considered her sad trade as business — completely divorced from her sexual drive, which was satisfied by her woman lover. Adverse domestic and economic conditions had driven these girls into the street.

When the women's movement succeeds in creating a situation in which occupants are open equally to all people according to their individual talents and capabilities, homosexual prostitutes would disappear, and a large percentage of the heterosexual girls who now turn to prostitution because of bad social conditions, could support themselves better and with more human dignity. They would prepare themselves for a profession early in life because they would be brought up to be independent. A girl who learns to deal with life at an early age will not be as apt to end up in the street as a girl who lives thoughtlessly with no understanding of the simplest and most natural aspects of life. In a certain sense, the struggle of the homosexual woman for social acceptance is also a struggle against prostitution, although I must emphasize the fact that this struggle could only result in a lessening of prostitution, not its eradication.

One must not forget that justice for Uranians in general would mean that a great number of homosexual men who are driven to prostitutes by their fear of detection would no longer find this necessary. This, of course, would result in a reduction of venereal disease, which though small would be valuable, for each single case in which syphilis or other venereal infection is avoided is a victory for the health of the people and the coming generation on whom rests the well-being and greatness of our fatherland.

The women's movement fights for the right of individuality and self-determination. It must admit that the alienating ban that society still places on Uranians suppresses this right; and therefore its responsibility is to join the homosexuals in their struggles, just as it actively assists unwed mothers, working women, and many others as they fight for freedom and right, battling against old, false, traditional concepts of a morality which is in actuality an immorality of the worst kind.

Just as woman is battling to win back the ancient human right which was taken from her by raw force, the Uranians have an innate, natural right to their love, which is as noble and pure as heterosexual love when the persons involved are good. There are good people among homosexuals just as there are among the so-called "normals."

I want most of all to avoid the appearance of having overestimated the Uranians. I can assure you, ladies and gentlemen, that I have not.

I recognize the faults and weaknesses of homosexuals too well, but I also know their good points and therefore can say: The Uranians are neither better nor worse than heterosexuals — they are not of different value, only of different kind.

In summary, I want to emphasize once more that the Uranian woman has played an important part in all aspects of our great women's movement. With her androgynous characteristics, she was often the one who initiated action because she felt most strongly the many, many injustices and hardships with which laws, society, and archaic customs treat women. Without the active support of the Uranian women, the women's movement would not be where it is today — this is an undisputable fact.

The women's movement and the homosexual rights movement have long traveled a dark path filled with innumerable obstacles. Now the light is gradually being turned on in human hearts, and it is becoming brighter for us. Not that the difficult fight for the rights of women and Uranians is over; we are still in the middle of strife in both instances, and many a heated battle will be fought, many a victim will fall because of false morality or an unfortunate law, before both movements attain their goal — individual liberation. Much sooner, both movements will reach the point when they will recognize that they have many mutual interests, when they will peacefully join hands in order to join forces in battle where it is necessary.

And if at first we find serious and difficult hours in store for us, we must not give up in cowardice, but must move courageously through the hostile forces, onward to the victory which is assured us. For the sun of understanding and truth has risen in the east, and no power of darkness can alter its radiant course — slowly it will rise higher and higher! Not today or tomorrow, but in the not too distant future, the women's movement and Uranians will raise their flags of victory!

Per aspera ad astra!

from   THE SCORPION

by Anna E. Weirauch

(Berlin, 1919)

Anna Weirauch's three-volume novel was published during the years 1919 to 1921. The first volume, from which this excerpt is taken, concerns the love relationship between Mette, a woman of twenty, and Olga, who is ten years older. While the love between the two women is shown to be enriching and constructive, they are separated by pressures from Mette's family and the medical establishment, which tries to convince Mette that homosexuality is sick and sinful. This volume ends in Olga's suicide after Mette's forced engagement to a man. The excerpt is noteworthy because it is one of the earliest lesbian lovemaking scenes written by a woman. The characters are shown here to reject butch/femme roles (which the medical establishment said lesbians must have), and they see their physical relationship to be tied to a spiritual one (which earlier male writers never recognized in their depictions of lesbian lovemaking).

Olga took off her skirt and blouse and wrapped herself in her kimono.

"Wonderful," she said. "Now I just wish I had warm feet and my hair pins out of my hair. Then I'd be wishlessly happy."

She rolled an armchair in front of the gas stove and began to unlace her high boots.

"Can I help you?" asked Mette, eager to serve.

"That's all we need!" Olga was ruffled.

"I would not even ask a maid to unlace my boots!"

"That's quite a different matter," Mette smiled. "It's a distinction one would begrudge a maid."

95

"You are crazy!" Again, Olga's face was suffused with a quick dark flush. Now she had peeled off her thin silk stockings, and she held her naked feet close to the flames. She lifted her arms and slowly pulled pin after pin from her hair until the heavy black strands cascaded down her back.

Mette jumped on a chair and turned off the gaslight.

"All right," she laughed, "now you can have someone paint you or else have yourself transformed immediately into an oleograph with a gold frame and hang yourself on this wall. Signature: *Au coin du feu*, or 'the witch,' or 'glowing embers,' or whatever else marvelous. How can anyone be so outrageously beautiful?!"

"Well!" Olga commented dryly, "you've certainly done a good job. Now we are out of matches."

"First of all, this lighting is good enough for me," Mette said and sat down on the floor in the reddish reflection of the fire, "and secondly we can always use a piece of paper if we need to light something. In case we can't find anything better, we can use a hundred mark bill. We certainly have enough of them. . . . My God, what exquisite feet you have . . . but they are still cold as ice!"

She put both hands around Olga's foot. It was so nobly shaped, it was so beautiful in line and color, just as if a master's hand had formed it from marble; but it also was as cold and heavy as marble.

Mette tried to warm it in her hands. She breathed on it, and then she couldn't resist the temptation: she put her lips on the cool, smooth white skin. Olga disengaged herself, jumped up, and ran to the window on the other side of the room.

"Olga," Mette said, frightened as she rose hesitantly. "What's the matter? What is wrong?"

There was no reply. Mette followed her. But when she reached the window and reached out to touch her, Olga ran toward the wall as if she were being chased.

She stood pressed into a corner, and Mette stepped in front of her.

The beautiful, pale face shone eerily through the dark. Her tense features expressed fear and menace simultaneously: she resembled a wounded, cornered animal, desperately fighting for life.

The expression of Olga's tightly set mouth, her dark burning eyes frightened Mette. Timidly, she laid her hand on Olga's arms, which her friend held crossed before her breast.

Olga flinched and pressed even deeper into the corner.

"Go away!" she said through clenched teeth. "Leave me alone!"

"You shouldn't stand barefooted on the cold floor," Mette begged, close to tears. "You are going to catch your death of cold. I don't want anything except that you sit by the stove. Then I can sleep in the hallway in front of the door, or else I can get another room, or I can jump out the window. But do come out of that corner. I can't bear to watch this any longer."

She grasped her shoulders, but Olga shook off her friend's hands.

"Do leave me alone!" she said angrily.

"Can't you see that you are torturing me unto death? How can any human being be so cruel?"

Her voice cracked, and suddenly tears streamed down her face.

Mette could no longer control herself. Her eyes, also, filled with tears.

"I don't understand you!" she said, her lips trembling. "If I'm so repugnant to you that you can't stand me, why are you here? Why do you even spend time with me? One can't be fond of a person whose presence means such torture! But I know why you can't stand me!"

"Why?" Olga asked surprised.

Silently Mette shook her head while she fought back the tears.

"Why is it that I supposedly can't stand you?" Olga insisted. "Answer! I want to know."

Mette still avoided looking at her. "Because I love you too much!" she said sadly and with bitterness. "It must be horrible to be loved by someone whom one does not love in return! Almost disgusting!"

"You silly," Olga said and very gently stroked Mette's hair.

"Don't," Mette said and withdrew from the stroking hand. "One shouldn't force oneself into anything."

Olga dropped her arm.

"Yes, one must force oneself," she said in a low voice, breathing with difficulty. "If I would not force myself now, I would so suffocate you with caresses that you would get scared to death and run away."

Mette felt her heart beat in her throat so that she could scarcely breathe. She tried to smile while tears still welled up in her eyes.

"Don't force yourself," she said, "I most certainly would not run away. But perhaps I would go insane with happiness!"

Olga slowly raised her white slender arms and put them around Mette's shoulders. Mette felt the pleasant pressure become firmer and firmer.

Now that Olga was standing on bare feet, their faces were almost at equal level.

They stared into each other's eyes, gravely and continuously, and felt the wild hammering of their hearts throughout their bodies.

Then they bent toward each other like two who were dying of thirst and joined mouth to mouth.

97

They could not let go of each other. Their kisses only increased their thirst for each other; close together, they walked through the room; they sat at the bed's edge tightly clasped in an embrace. They dropped their clothes carelessly and left them lying on the floor.

The coarse, damp sheets breathed coolness. They barely felt it, for their blood boiled in their young bodies.

They pressed together as if they wanted to enter into each other, melt into each other, become one.

Their slender, supple limbs became entwined like jungle trees.

They were silent, but they heard each other's hearts pound like furious music and their breaths came faster and faster.

Their bodies reared up against each other like wild animals shaking the bars of their cages. Nails dug into smooth skin, and teeth bit into taut muscles.

And then they lay nestled close to each other like children tired from playing, and their lips brushed each other's eyelids and cheeks as softly as butterfly wings, as swaying blossoms.

"My little one," Olga said, and bells were ringing in her voice. "My beautiful, my dear one!"

"Oh you!" said Mette. "You miracle from heaven, who are you? Are you a wild animal . . . or a god . . . or the spirit of a white orchid?"

"I don't know," said Olga. "I think I am a god. But only an hour ago I was a poor, tortured animal. Aren't you proud, little girl, that you can work such miracles?"

"I wish I could work miracles," said Mette longingly.

A bitter smile flashed across Olga's mouth.

"You'd change me into a man, wouldn't you?" she said.

"Oh my God!" Mette exclaimed and wrapped both arms around her, full of fright. "Never, never, never! . . . But if I could work miracles, I would let this night never end. I would let it last all eternity!"

The red shine of the copper behind the gas flame cast the outline of the room into mellow twilight. The pointed little flames were trembling, and the faded spot on the colored, worn carpet trembled in accord.

Olga propped herself on her elbows and cupped her face in one hand. Strands of black hair trickled through her white fingers. From her pale face her dark eyes shone like two stars with immense majesty and clarity.

"Eternal!" she said in a low voice. "All that is godlike is eternal. Don't you feel that this night belongs to God? Time is the devil's invention. Satan invented transiency in order to make humans rebel

98

against God. But God remained eternal, and God's glory remains eternal. So then Satan invented all manner of other things: disease, pain, vermin, and money . . . above all money. And then there was time also and transience, and they could no longer be undone. And now they cling to all inventions of the devil. But whatever is godlike is eternal. New happiness forever extinguishes old pain as if it had never existed. But the happiness remains. And no pain can take it away. — I would die of shame if I thought that our happiness is due only to the vibration of nerve endings in the skin of our hands. Don't you feel that something happened to your soul which will stay beyond death? Don't you feel that this hour has changed you far more than the little matter of dying can change you?"

"Yes," Mette replied. "And more than that little matter of being born also. Today was the day of my birth, and not twenty years ago. Now I can for the first time consciously say: I am alive!"

"We are alive!" Olga seized her with a shout of joy that sounded like the exultant call of a wild bird.

"We are alive, sweetheart. We'll live forever, forever, forever!"

A few of the publications of
THE NAIAD PRESS, INC.
P.O. Box 10543 ● Tallahassee, Florida 32302
Phone (904) 539-5965
Mail orders welcome. Please include 15% postage.

VIRAGO by Karen Marie Christa Minns. 208 pp. Darsen has
chosen Ginny. ISBN 0-941483-56-8 $8.95

WILDERNESS TREK by Dorothy Tell. 192 pp. Six women on
vacation learning "new" skills. ISBN 0-941483-60-6   8.95

MURDER BY THE BOOK by Pat Welch. 256 pp. A Helen
Black Mystery. First in a series. ISBN 0-941483-59-2   8.95

BERRIGAN by Vicki P. McConnell. 176 pp. Youthful Lesbian–
romantic, idealistic Berrigan. ISBN 0-941483-55-X   8.95

LESBIANS IN GERMANY by Lillian Faderman & B. Eriksson.
128 pp. Fiction, poetry, essays. ISBN 0-941483-62-2   8.95

THE BEVERLY MALIBU by Katherine V. Forrest. 288 pp. A
Kate Delafield Mystery. 3rd in a series. ISBN 0-941483-47-9   16.95

THERE'S SOMETHING I'VE BEEN MEANING TO TELL
YOU Ed. by Loralee MacPike. 288 pp. Gay men and lesbians
coming out to their children. ISBN 0-941483-44-4   9.95
ISBN 0-941483-54-1   16.95

LIFTING BELLY by Gertrude Stein. Ed. by Rebecca Mark. 104
pp. Erotic poetry. ISBN 0-941483-51-7   8.95
ISBN 0-941483-53-3   14.95

ROSE PENSKI by Roz Perry. 192 pp. Adult lovers in a long-term
relationship. ISBN 0-941483-37-1   8.95

AFTER THE FIRE by Jane Rule. 256 pp. Warm, human novel
by this incomparable author. ISBN 0-941483-45-2   8.95

SUE SLATE, PRIVATE EYE by Lee Lynch. 176 pp. The gay
folk of Peacock Alley are *all* cats. ISBN 0-941483-52-5   8.95

CHRIS by Randy Salem. 224 pp. Golden oldie. Handsome Chris
and her adventures. ISBN 0-941483-42-8   8.95

THREE WOMEN by March Hastings. 232 pp. Golden oldie. A
triangle among wealthy sophisticates. ISBN 0-941483-43-6   8.95

RICE AND BEANS by Valeria Taylor. 232 pp. Love and
romance on poverty row. ISBN 0-941483-41-X   8.95

PLEASURES by Robbi Sommers. 204 pp. Unprecedented
eroticism. ISBN 0-941483-49-5   8.95

EDGEWISE by Camarin Grae. 372 pp. Spellbinding
adventure. ISBN 0-941483-19-3   9.95

FATAL REUNION by Claire McNab. 216 pp. 2nd Det. Inspec.
Carol Ashton mystery. ISBN 0-941483-40-1   8.95

KEEP TO ME STRANGER by Sarah Aldridge. 372 pp. Romance
set in a department store dynasty.   ISBN 0-941483-38-X   9.95

HEARTSCAPE by Sue Gambill. 204 pp. American lesbian in
Portugal.   ISBN 0-941483-33-9   8.95

IN THE BLOOD by Lauren Wright Douglas. 252 pp. Lesbian
science fiction adventure fantasy   ISBN 0-941483-22-3   8.95

THE BEE'S KISS by Shirley Verel. 216 pp. Delicate, delicious
romance.   ISBN 0-941483-36-3   8.95

RAGING MOTHER MOUNTAIN by Pat Emmerson. 264 pp.
Furosa Firechild's adventures in Wonderland. ISBN 0-941483-35-5   8.95

IN EVERY PORT by Karin Kallmaker. 228 pp. Jessica's sexy,
adventuresome travels.   ISBN 0-941483-37-7   8.95

OF LOVE AND GLORY by Evelyn Kennedy. 192 pp. Exciting
WWII romance.   ISBN 0-941483-32-0   8.95

CLICKING STONES by Nancy Tyler Glenn. 288 pp. Love
transcending time.   ISBN 0-941483-31-2   8.95

SURVIVING SISTERS by Gail Pass. 252 pp. Powerful love
story.   ISBN 0-941483-16-9   8.95

SOUTH OF THE LINE by Catherine Ennis. 216 pp. Civil War
adventure.   ISBN 0-941483-29-0   8.95

WOMAN PLUS WOMAN by Dolores Klaich. 300 pp. Supurb
Lesbian overview.   ISBN 0-941483-28-2   9.95

SLOW DANCING AT MISS POLLY'S by Sheila Ortiz Taylor.
96 pp. Lesbian Poetry   ISBN 0-941483-30-4   7.95

DOUBLE DAUGHTER by Vicki P. McConnell. 216 pp. A Nyla
Wade Mystery, third in the series.   ISBN 0-941483-26-6   8.95

HEAVY GILT by Delores Klaich. 192 pp. Lesbian detective/
disappearing homophobes/upper class gay society.

        ISBN 0-941483-25-8   8.95

THE FINER GRAIN by Denise Ohio. 216 pp. Brilliant young
college lesbian novel.   ISBN 0-941483-11-8   8.95

THE AMAZON TRAIL by Lee Lynch. 216 pp. Life, travel & lore
of famous lesbian author.   ISBN 0-941483-27-4   8.95

HIGH CONTRAST by Jessie Lattimore. 264 pp. Women of the
Crystal Palace.   ISBN 0-941483-17-7   8.95

OCTOBER OBSESSION by Meredith More. Josie's rich, secret
Lesbian life.   ISBN 0-941483-18-5   8.95

LESBIAN CROSSROADS by Ruth Baetz. 276 pp. Contemporary
Lesbian lives.   ISBN 0-941483-21-5   9.95

BEFORE STONEWALL: THE MAKING OF A GAY AND
LESBIAN COMMUNITY by Andrea Weiss & Greta Schiller.
96 pp., 25 illus.   ISBN 0-941483-20-7   7.95

WE WALK THE BACK OF THE TIGER by Patricia A. Murphy.
192 pp. Romantic Lesbian novel/beginning women's movement.
ISBN 0-941483-13-4   8.95

SUNDAY'S CHILD by Joyce Bright. 216 pp. Lesbian athletics, at
last the novel about sports.   ISBN 0-941483-12-6   8.95

OSTEN'S BAY by Zenobia N. Vole. 204 pp. Sizzling adventure
romance set on Bonaire.   ISBN 0-941483-15-0   8.95

LESSONS IN MURDER by Claire McNab. 216 pp. 1st Det. Inspec.
Carol Ashton mystery — erotic tension!.   ISBN 0-941483-14-2   8.95

YELLOWTHROAT by Penny Hayes. 240 pp. Margarita, bandit,
kidnaps Julia.   ISBN 0-941483-10-X   8.95

SAPPHISTRY: THE BOOK OF LESBIAN SEXUALITY by
Pat Califia. 3d edition, revised. 208 pp.   ISBN 0-941483-24-X   8.95

CHERISHED LOVE by Evelyn Kennedy. 192 pp. Erotic
Lesbian love story.   ISBN 0-941483-08-8   8.95

LAST SEPTEMBER by Helen R. Hull. 208 pp. Six stories & a
glorious novella.   ISBN 0-941483-09-6   8.95

THE SECRET IN THE BIRD by Camarin Grae. 312 pp. Striking,
psychological suspense novel.   ISBN 0-941483-05-3   8.95

TO THE LIGHTNING by Catherine Ennis. 208 pp. Romantic
Lesbian 'Robinson Crusoe' adventure.   ISBN 0-941483-06-1   8.95

THE OTHER SIDE OF VENUS by Shirley Verel. 224 pp.
Luminous, romantic love story.   ISBN 0-941483-07-X   8.95

DREAMS AND SWORDS by Katherine V. Forrest. 192 pp.
Romantic, erotic, imaginative stories.   ISBN 0-941483-03-7   8.95

MEMORY BOARD by Jane Rule. 336 pp. Memorable novel
about an aging Lesbian couple.   ISBN 0-941483-02-9   9.95

THE ALWAYS ANONYMOUS BEAST by Lauren Wright
Douglas. 224 pp. A Caitlin Reese mystery. First in a series.
ISBN 0-941483-04-5   8.95

SEARCHING FOR SPRING by Patricia A. Murphy. 224 pp.
Novel about the recovery of love.   ISBN 0-941483-00-2   8.95

DUSTY'S QUEEN OF HEARTS DINER by Lee Lynch. 240 pp.
Romantic blue-collar novel.   ISBN 0-941483-01-0   8.95

PARENTS MATTER by Ann Muller. 240 pp. Parents'
relationships with Lesbian daughters and gay sons.
ISBN 0-930044-91-6   9.95

THE PEARLS by Shelley Smith. 176 pp. Passion and fun in
the Caribbean sun.   ISBN 0-930044-93-2   7.95

MAGDALENA by Sarah Aldridge. 352 pp. Epic Lesbian novel
set on three continents.   ISBN 0-930044-99-1   8.95

THE BLACK AND WHITE OF IT by Ann Allen Shockley.
144 pp. Short stories.   ISBN 0-930044-96-7   7.95

SAY JESUS AND COME TO ME by Ann Allen Shockley. 288
pp. Contemporary romance.   ISBN 0-930044-98-3   8.95

LOVING HER by Ann Allen Shockley. 192 pp. Romantic love
story.   ISBN 0-930044-97-5   7.95

MURDER AT THE NIGHTWOOD BAR by Katherine V.
Forrest. 240 pp. A Kate Delafield mystery. Second in a series.
                                          ISBN 0-930044-92-4   8.95

ZOE'S BOOK by Gail Pass. 224 pp. Passionate, obsessive love
story.   ISBN 0-930044-95-9   7.95

WINGED DANCER by Camarin Grae. 228 pp. Erotic Lesbian
adventure story.   ISBN 0-930044-88-6   8.95

PAZ by Camarin Grae. 336 pp. Romantic Lesbian adventurer
with the power to change the world.   ISBN 0-930044-89-4   8.95

SOUL SNATCHER by Camarin Grae. 224 pp. A puzzle, an
adventure, a mystery — Lesbian romance.   ISBN 0-930044-90-8   8.95

THE LOVE OF GOOD WOMEN by Isabel Miller. 224 pp.
Long-awaited new novel by the author of the beloved *Patience
and Sarah.*   ISBN 0-930044-81-9   8.95

THE HOUSE AT PELHAM FALLS by Brenda Weathers. 240
pp. Suspenseful Lesbian ghost story.   ISBN 0-930044-79-7   7.95

HOME IN YOUR HANDS by Lee Lynch. 240 pp. More stories
from the author of *Old Dyke Tales.*   ISBN 0-930044-80-0   7.95

EACH HAND A MAP by Anita Skeen. 112 pp. Real-life poems
that touch us all.   ISBN 0-930044-82-7   6.95

SURPLUS by Sylvia Stevenson. 342 pp. A classic early Lesbian
novel.   ISBN 0-930044-78-9   7.95

PEMBROKE PARK by Michelle Martin. 256 pp. Derring-do
and daring romance in Regency England.   ISBN 0-930044-77-0   7.95

THE LONG TRAIL by Penny Hayes. 248 pp. Vivid adventures
of two women in love in the old west.   ISBN 0-930044-76-2   8.95

HORIZON OF THE HEART by Shelley Smith. 192 pp. Hot
romance in summertime New England.   ISBN 0-930044-75-4   7.95

AN EMERGENCE OF GREEN by Katherine V. Forrest. 288
pp. Powerful novel of sexual discovery.   ISBN 0-930044-69-X   8.95

THE LESBIAN PERIODICALS INDEX edited by Claire
Potter. 432 pp. Author & subject index.   ISBN 0-930044-74-6   29.95

DESERT OF THE HEART by Jane Rule. 224 pp. A classic;
basis for the movie *Desert Hearts.*   ISBN 0-930044-73-8   7.95

SPRING FORWARD/FALL BACK by Sheila Ortiz Taylor.
288 pp. Literary novel of timeless love. ISBN 0-930044-70-3   7.95

FOR KEEPS by Elisabeth Nonas. 144 pp. Contemporary novel
about losing and finding love.   ISBN 0-930044-71-1   7.95

TORCHLIGHT TO VALHALLA by Gale Wilhelm. 128 pp.
Classic novel by a great Lesbian writer.   ISBN 0-930044-68-1   7.95

LESBIAN NUNS: BREAKING SILENCE edited by Rosemary
Curb and Nancy Manahan. 432 pp. Unprecedented autobiographies
of religious life.   ISBN 0-930044-62-2   9.95

THE SWASHBUCKLER by Lee Lynch. 288 pp. Colorful novel
set in Greenwich Village in the sixties.   ISBN 0-930044-66-5   8.95

MISFORTUNE'S FRIEND by Sarah Aldridge. 320 pp. Histori-
cal Lesbian novel set on two continents.   ISBN 0-930044-67-3   7.95

A STUDIO OF ONE'S OWN by Ann Stokes. Edited by
Dolores Klaich. 128 pp. Autobiography.   ISBN 0-930044-64-9   7.95

SEX VARIANT WOMEN IN LITERATURE by Jeannette
Howard Foster. 448 pp. Literary history.   ISBN 0-930044-65-7   8.95

A HOT-EYED MODERATE by Jane Rule. 252 pp. Hard-hitting
essays on gay life; writing; art.   ISBN 0-930044-57-6   7.95

INLAND PASSAGE AND OTHER STORIES by Jane Rule.
288 pp. Wide-ranging new collection.   ISBN 0-930044-56-8   7.95

WE TOO ARE DRIFTING by Gale Wilhelm. 128 pp. Timeless
Lesbian novel, a masterpiece.   ISBN 0-930044-61-4   6.95

AMATEUR CITY by Katherine V. Forrest. 224 pp. A Kate
Delafield mystery. First in a series.   ISBN 0-930044-55-X   7.95

THE SOPHIE HOROWITZ STORY by Sarah Schulman. 176
pp. Engaging novel of madcap intrigue.   ISBN 0-930044-54-1   7.95

THE BURNTON WIDOWS by Vickie P. McConnell. 272 pp. A
Nyla Wade mystery, second in the series.   ISBN 0-930044-52-5   7.95

OLD DYKE TALES by Lee Lynch. 224 pp. Extraordinary
stories of our diverse Lesbian lives.   ISBN 0-930044-51-7   8.95

DAUGHTERS OF A CORAL DAWN by Katherine V. Forrest.
240 pp. Novel set in a Lesbian new world.   ISBN 0-930044-50-9   7.95

THE PRICE OF SALT by Claire Morgan. 288 pp. A milestone
novel, a beloved classic.   ISBN 0-930044-49-5   8.95

AGAINST THE SEASON by Jane Rule. 224 pp. Luminous,
complex novel of interrelationships.   ISBN 0-930044-48-7   8.95

LOVERS IN THE PRESENT AFTERNOON by Kathleen
Fleming. 288 pp. A novel about recovery and growth.
          ISBN 0-930044-46-0   8.95

TOOTHPICK HOUSE by Lee Lynch. 264 pp. Love between
two Lesbians of different classes.   ISBN 0-930044-45-2   7.95

MADAME AURORA by Sarah Aldridge. 256 pp. Historical
novel featuring a charismatic "seer."   ISBN 0-930044-44-4   7.95

CURIOUS WINE by Katherine V. Forrest. 176 pp. Passionate
Lesbian love story, a best-seller.   ISBN 0-930044-43-6   8.95

BLACK LESBIAN IN WHITE AMERICA by Anita Cornwell.
141 pp. Stories, essays, autobiography.   ISBN 0-930044-41-X   7.50

CONTRACT WITH THE WORLD by Jane Rule. 340 pp.
Powerful, panoramic novel of gay life.   ISBN 0-930044-28-2   9.95

MRS. PORTER'S LETTER by Vicki P. McConnell. 224 pp.
The first Nyla Wade mystery.   ISBN 0-930044-29-0   7.95

TO THE CLEVELAND STATION by Carol Anne Douglas.
192 pp. Interracial Lesbian love story.   ISBN 0-930044-27-4   6.95

THE NESTING PLACE by Sarah Aldridge. 224 pp. A
three-woman triangle—love conquers all!   ISBN 0-930044-26-6   7.95

THIS IS NOT FOR YOU by Jane Rule. 284 pp. A letter to a
beloved is also an intricate novel.   ISBN 0-930044-25-8   8.95

FAULTLINE by Sheila Ortiz Taylor. 140 pp. Warm, funny,
literate story of a startling family.   ISBN 0-930044-24-X   6.95

THE LESBIAN IN LITERATURE by Barbara Grier. 3d ed.
Foreword by Maida Tilchen. 240 pp. Comprehensive bibliography.
Literary ratings; rare photos.   ISBN 0-930044-23-1   7.95

ANNA'S COUNTRY by Elizabeth Lang. 208 pp. A woman
finds her Lesbian identity.   ISBN 0-930044-19-3   6.95

PRISM by Valerie Taylor. 158 pp. A love affair between two
women in their sixties.   ISBN 0-930044-18-5   6.95

BLACK LESBIANS: AN ANNOTATED BIBLIOGRAPHY
compiled by J. R. Roberts. Foreword by Barbara Smith. 112 pp.
Award-winning bibliography.   ISBN 0-930044-21-5   5.95

THE MARQUISE AND THE NOVICE by Victoria Ramstetter.
108 pp. A Lesbian Gothic novel.   ISBN 0-930044-16-9   6.95

OUTLANDER by Jane Rule. 207 pp. Short stories and essays
by one of our finest writers.   ISBN 0-930044-17-7   8.95

ALL TRUE LOVERS by Sarah Aldridge. 292 pp. Romantic
novel set in the 1930s and 1940s.   ISBN 0-930044-10-X   7.95

A WOMAN APPEARED TO ME by Renee Vivien. 65 pp. A
classic; translated by Jeannette H. Foster.   ISBN 0-930044-06-1   5.00

CYTHEREA'S BREATH by Sarah Aldridge. 240 pp. Romantic
novel about women's entrance into medicine.
          ISBN 0-930044-02-9   6.95

TOTTIE by Sarah Aldridge. 181 pp. Lesbian romance in the
turmoil of the sixties.   ISBN 0-930044-01-0   6.95

THE LATECOMER by Sarah Aldridge. 107 pp. A delicate love
story.   ISBN 0-930044-00-2   6.95